CONTENT ESSENTIALS™
for
Science

Vocabulary

Content

Literacy

Mc Graw Hill **Wright Group**

The **McGraw·Hill** Companies

www.WrightGroup.com

 **Wright Group**

Send all inquiries to:
Wright Group/McGraw-Hill
P.O. Box 812960
Chicago, IL 60681

ISBN 978-1-4045-6729-0
MHID 1-4045-6729-1

1 2 3 4 5 6 7 8 9 QWD 14 13 12 11 10 09 08

The **McGraw·Hill** Companies

Author

Margarita Calderón, Ph.D.
Senior Research Scientist and Professor
Johns Hopkins University

Content Consultant

James A. Shymansky, Ph.D.
E. Desmond Lee Professor of Science
    Education
University of Missouri–St. Louis

Reviewers

Amy Diedrichsen Bates
Curriculum Specialist
Plano Independent School District
Plano, Texas

Lillian Vega Castaneda, Ed.D.
Professor, Language, Culture, and Literacy
California State University
Channel Islands
Camarillo, California

Susan Greca
Director of Second Language Programs
Freeport Public Schools
Freeport, New York

Elizabeth Jiménez
English Learner Consultant
GEMAS Consulting Co.
Pomona, California

Sandra Ann Madriaga
Supervisor of World Languages,
    English as a Second Language
    and High-Ability Programs
Evansville-Vanderburgh School Corporation
Evansville, Indiana

Janie Perez Martin
Physics Instructor
Southwest Independent School District
San Antonio, Texas

Vyagale D. Maryland
Title III/ESL & Languages Other than
    English Specialist
Montgomery Public Schools
Montgomery, Alabama

Ann L. Rifleman
Teacher
Mesa Unified School District
Mesa, Arizona

Elma Alicia Ruiz
Humanities Coordinator
Denver Public Schools, Department of
    Teaching and Learning
Denver, Colorado

Linda Thompson, Ed.D.
Director of Curriculum, Instruction,
    and Assessment
Carmel Clay Schools
Carmel, Indiana

Contents

HOW TO USE THIS BOOK **10**

Previewing Lessons 12

Learning Academic Vocabulary 13

Part One Science Essentials 14

🍃 LIFE SCIENCE 16

Living Things 18

What Plants Need 20

Parts of a Plant........................... 22

Kinds of Plants............................ 24

How Plants Are Adapted 26

Habitats 28

Types of Animals 34

How Animals Are Adapted 42

Endangered Animals 44

Food Energy 46

The Food Chain 48

Life Cycles................................... 50

EARTH SCIENCE **54**

Rocks and Minerals....................... 56
Soil 58
How Earth Changes 60
Fossils.. 62
Landforms 64
Water.. 66
Pollution.. 68
Recycling 70
The Sun and Stars........................ 72
Day and Night.............................. 74
The Seasons.................................. 76
The Solar System.......................... 78
Weather.. 80
Measuring the Weather 82
The Water Cycle 84
Storms.. 86

PHYSICAL SCIENCE **90**

Matter 92
States of Matter 94
Changing Matter 98
Energy 100
Heat 102
Light 104
Sound 106
Motion 108
Force 110
Gravity 112
Friction 114
Simple Machines 116
Magnets 118
Technology 120

STUDYING SCIENCE **122**

Science Process Skills 124
Using Science Methods 132

Part Two Literacy Essentials 136

READING SCIENCE 138

Science Textbooks 140
Magazines and Newspapers 142
Internet 144
Parts of a Textbook 146
Textbook Features 150

COMPREHENSION 154

Comparing and Contrasting 156
Predicting 158
Determining Important Information 160
Summarizing 162
Making Inferences 164
Visualizing 166
Asking and Answering Questions 168
Monitoring Comprehension 170
Identifying Cause-Effect 172
Making Connections 174

UNDERSTANDING LANGUAGE **176**

Prefixes and Suffixes 178
Cognates 180

WRITING FOR SCIENCE **182**

Taking Notes 184
Organizing Ideas 186
Writing About Ideas 188

SCIENCE REFERENCES **190**

Science Tools 192
Science Safety 194

GLOSSARY **196**

Credits 207

How to Use This Book

Your book has two parts. You can use the first part to learn about science topics. If you need help reading or writing about science, use the second part.

Part One Science Essentials

LIFE SCIENCE Life science is the study of living things. You will learn about many types of living things, and how they live.

EARTH SCIENCE Earth science is the study of our planet Earth. It includes facts about rocks, weather, water, and space.

PHYSICAL SCIENCE Physical science is the study of matter and energy. You will learn how energy makes matter change or move.

STUDYING SCIENCE Science is about asking and answering questions. These lessons show you how scientists solve problems.

Part Two Literacy Essentials

READING SCIENCE The lessons in this section show you how to use text features to help you read.

COMPREHENSION These lessons teach you strategies and skills for reading.

UNDERSTANDING LANGUAGE This section helps you learn phrases and words in the English language.

WRITING FOR SCIENCE The lessons in this section show you how to write a science report.

Previewing Lessons

Each lesson has the same text features: an Essential Idea, photographs, labels, and Why It Matters. These features will help you understand the lesson.

Essential Idea
The Essential Idea tells you what the lesson is all about.

photographs
Photographs help you visualize the topic.

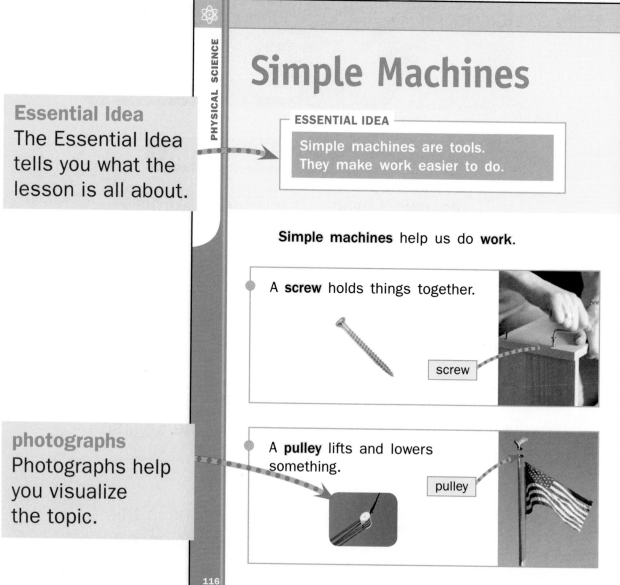

PHYSICAL SCIENCE

Simple Machines

ESSENTIAL IDEA

Simple machines are tools. They make work easier to do.

Simple machines help us do **work**.

A **screw** holds things together.

screw

A **pulley** lifts and lowers something.

pulley

116

12

Learning Academic Vocabulary

You need to know academic vocabulary, or words used in school subjects, to learn. Each lesson highlights the words you will need to understand ideas in science.

key words Special print shows you the academic vocabulary words.

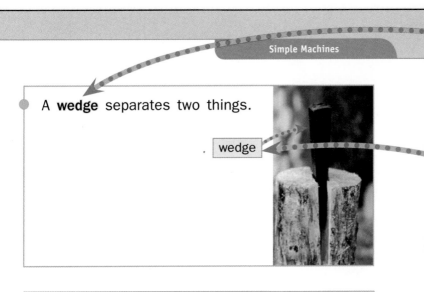

Simple Machines

A **wedge** separates two things.

wedge

labels Labels on pictures help you name what is in the picture.

A **lever** moves or lifts something.

lever

Why It Matters Why It Matters connects the topic to your life.

WHY IT MATTERS

You use simple machines to do work.
You use tools every day.

117

Part One

Science Essentials

In this part of the book, you will learn all about the basics of science.

 LIFE SCIENCE 16

Life science is the study of living things. You will learn about many types of living things and how they live.

🌍 **EARTH SCIENCE** 54

Earth science is the study of our planet Earth. It includes rocks, weather, water, and space.

⚛ **PHYSICAL SCIENCE** 90

Physical science is the study of matter and energy. You will learn how energy makes matter change or move.

 STUDYING SCIENCE 122

Science is about asking and answering questions. These lessons show you how scientists solve problems.

Life Science

Living Things

ESSENTIAL IDEA

Living things are alive. They grow.

Plants and **animals** are living things.

Living things change and grow. They need food, water, and air to **live**.

trees

animal

water

rocks

Nonliving things do not grow. They do not need food, water, and air.

Living Things	Nonliving Things
animals 	rocks 
trees	water

WHY IT MATTERS

You are a living thing.
You need food, water, and air to live.

What Plants Need

ESSENTIAL IDEA

Plants need water, sunlight, and air.

Plants make their own food to **survive**. They use water, sunlight, and air to make food.

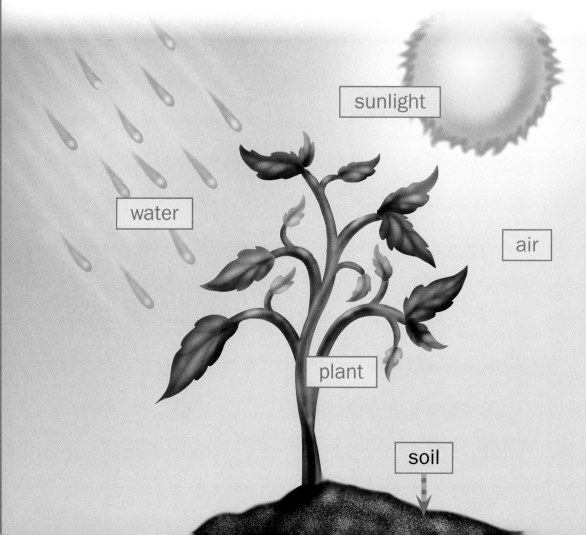

sunlight

water

air

plant

soil

Sunlight gives plants **energy** to make food.

Plants take in water from the **soil**.

sunlight

air

Things Plants Need

water

WHY IT MATTERS

Like plants, you need air, water, and light to live.

21

Parts of a Plant

┌─ **ESSENTIAL IDEA** ──────────────┐
│ A stem, leaves, flowers, and roots │
│ are the basic parts of most plants. │
└────────────────────────────────────┘

A plant has different **parts**. Most plants have a **stem**, **flowers**, **leaves**, and **roots**.

flower

leaves

stem

Parts of Plants

Each part of the plant has a job.

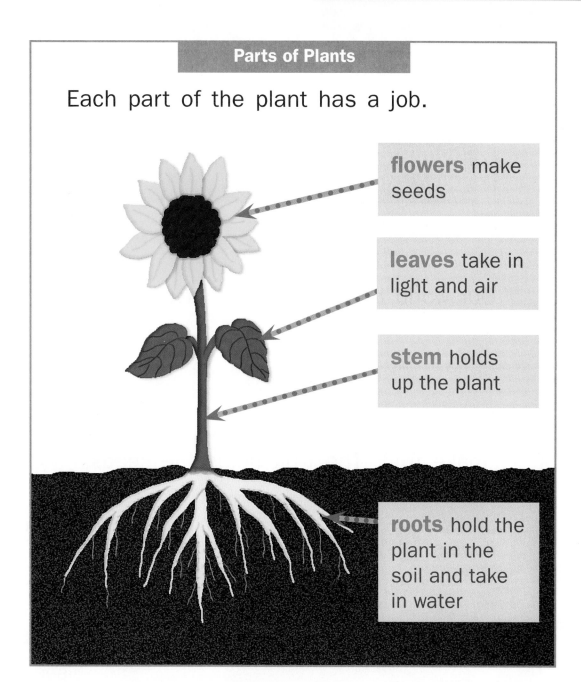

flowers make seeds

leaves take in light and air

stem holds up the plant

roots hold the plant in the soil and take in water

WHY IT MATTERS

You take in water in a different way than plants do.

Kinds of Plants

ESSENTIAL IDEA

Some plants have flowers. Some have cones.

Our world has many **kinds** of plants.

Plants with Flowers

Some plants have **flowers**. The flowers make **fruit**. The fruit holds the **seeds**.

flowers

apple tree

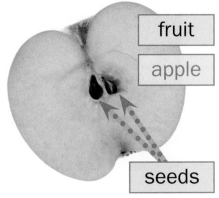

fruit

apple

seeds

▲ The seeds inside an apple help make new apple trees.

Plants with Cones

Some plants have **cones**. Cones have seeds like flowers do.

cone

seeds

▲ A pine tree stores its seeds in a pinecone.

WHY IT MATTERS

You eat fruit that has seeds.

25

How Plants Are Adapted

ESSENTIAL IDEA

Plants are adapted to their environments.

Plants can live in different places. Plants are **adapted** to fit their **environment**.

• A cactus lives in a hot environment.

The thick stem of a cactus holds water.

cactus

A water lily lives in water.

A water lily has leaves that float on the water.

water lily

Pine trees live where it is cold and dry.

Some plants freeze in cold weather. Pine trees do not.

pine tree

WHY IT MATTERS

You are adapted to survive in your environment.

Habitats

A **habitat** is a home for living things.

A habitat meets the **needs** of living things. It gives plants and animals things like food, water, and air.

squirrel

The squirrel gets the things it needs from its habitat.

Forest

A **forest** is a kind of habitat.

Many kinds of trees can grow in a forest.

▲ A forest habitat has sun, food, and water.

LIFE SCIENCE

Desert

A **desert** habitat is very dry. A desert does not get much rain.

▲
Some deserts are hot.

▲
Some deserts are cold.

Grassland

A **grassland** is a habitat with lots of grass. A grassland does not have many trees.

A grassland has few trees.

Rain Forest

A **rain forest** is a forest with lots of rain. Most rain forests are **tropical**, or hot.

bird

rain forest

▲
Many different plants and animals live in the rain forest.

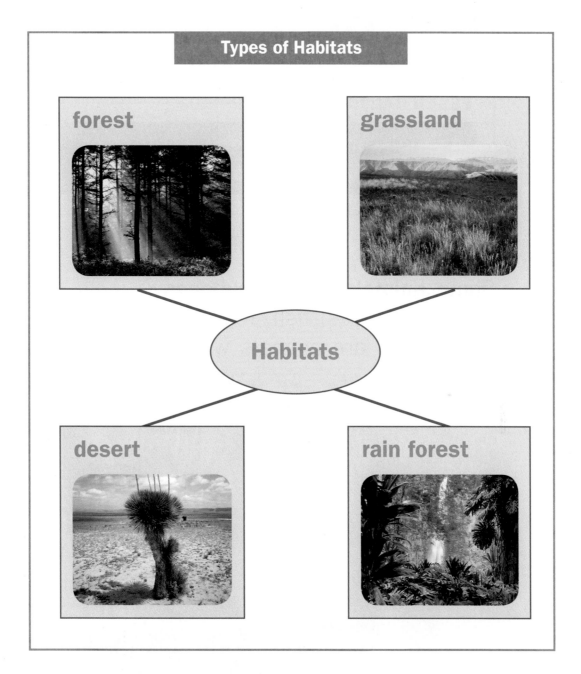

Types of Habitats

forest

grassland

Habitats

desert

rain forest

WHY IT MATTERS

> You live in a habitat.
> Your habitat meets your needs.

Types of Animals

ESSENTIAL IDEA

Animals are grouped by whether or not they have backbones.

Some **animals** have **backbones**. Mammals, birds, fish, reptiles, and amphibians are animals with backbones.

backbone

▲
A koala has a backbone.

Mammals

Mammals are **warm-blooded**.

A mammal has **lungs** to breathe and **hair**. Baby mammals get milk from their mothers.

A koala is a mammal.

LIFE SCIENCE

Birds

All **birds** have **wings**. But not all birds fly!
Birds have **feathers** on their wings.

▲
An eagle has wings to fly.

Fish

Fish live only in water. They use **gills** to **breathe** under water.

Fish have **fins** to help them swim. They are also covered with **scales**.

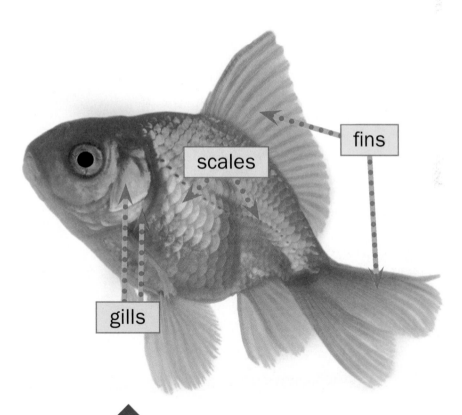

This goldfish swims in water.

LIFE SCIENCE

Reptiles

Reptiles are **cold-blooded**. Their bodies are the same **temperature** as the outside temperature.

Reptiles are covered with scales.

snake

▲
Reptiles live mostly on land.

Amphibians

Frogs and toads are kinds of **amphibians**.
Most amphibians are born in the water.
As adults, many amphibians live on **land**.

Life of a Frog

1 **born in water**
A tadpole is a baby frog. It is born in the water.

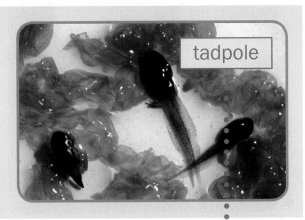

tadpole

2 **live on land**
The frog grows up. It lives on land.

frog

Animals Without Backbones

Most animals do not have **backbones**.

jellyfish

octopus

Some animals have hard **shells**.
The shells keep the animals safe.

snail

shell

Insects do not have backbones. All insects have six legs and three body parts.

leg

body

ant

Types of Animals	
Animals with backbones	**Animals without backbones**
koala	octopus
eagle	jellyfish
goldfish	snail
snake	ant
frog	

WHY IT MATTERS

You have a backbone.
You are a mammal.

How Animals Are Adapted

ESSENTIAL IDEA

Animals are adapted to live in their environments.

Animals have **features** that help them stay alive. Animals are **adapted** to their environment.

- Some animals **store** food energy in their bodies. They can go a long time without food or water.

camel

A camel is adapted to the desert.

Many animals look like the place they live in. This helps them **hide** from danger.

This fish is hard to find in its environment.

WHY IT MATTERS

You are adapted to live in your environment.

Endangered Animals

ESSENTIAL IDEA

Animals can become threatened, endangered, or extinct.

Sometimes animals begin to die off. There are fewer of that kind of animal. That animal becomes **threatened**.

If even more animals die off, that kind of animal becomes **endangered**.

panda

◄ The giant panda is endangered.

If all the animals die, that kind of animal is **extinct**. Extinct means there are none left.

The dodo bird is extinct. ▶

Threatened, Endangered, and Extinct

Threatened
Begin to die off

grizzly bear

Endangered
Very few left

jaguar

Extinct
All have died off

dodo

WHY IT MATTERS

Humans are not endangered.
You can help protect animals.

Food Energy

ESSENTIAL IDEA

All plants and animals need energy. They get energy from food.

Plants make their own food using energy from the Sun. They are **producers**.

Animals are **consumers**. Consumers get energy from living things they eat.

consumers

deer

producers

grass

Types of Consumers

There are different kinds of consumers.

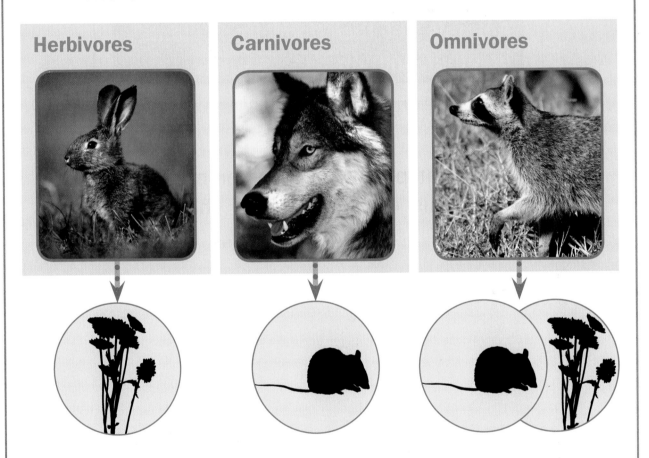

Herbivores

Carnivores

Omnivores

Herbivores eat only plants. **Carnivores** eat meat. **Omnivores** eat both plants and meat.

WHY IT MATTERS

You are a consumer.

The Food Chain

Animals eat plants or other animals to survive. This is called a **food chain**.

water plant

tadpole

The water plant makes food.

The tadpole eats the plant.

A **predator** is an animal that eats another animal. The animal that it eats is called its **prey**.

WHY IT MATTERS

> You eat living things to survive.
> You are part of a food chain.

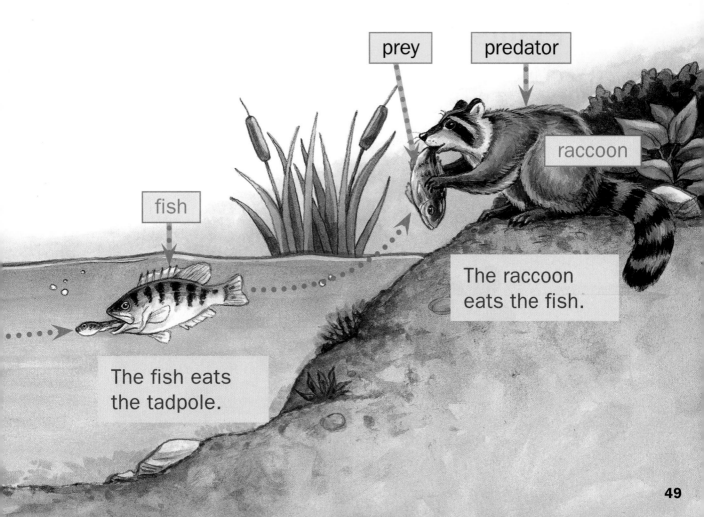

prey

predator

raccoon

fish

The raccoon eats the fish.

The fish eats the tadpole.

LIFE SCIENCE

Life Cycles

ESSENTIAL IDEA

Living things grow. They change in a life cycle.

Animals and plants change as they grow. The changes are called the **life cycle**.

Plants

Plants start as **seeds**. They grow up. They make more seeds.

seed

seedling

The Life Cycle of a Bean Plant

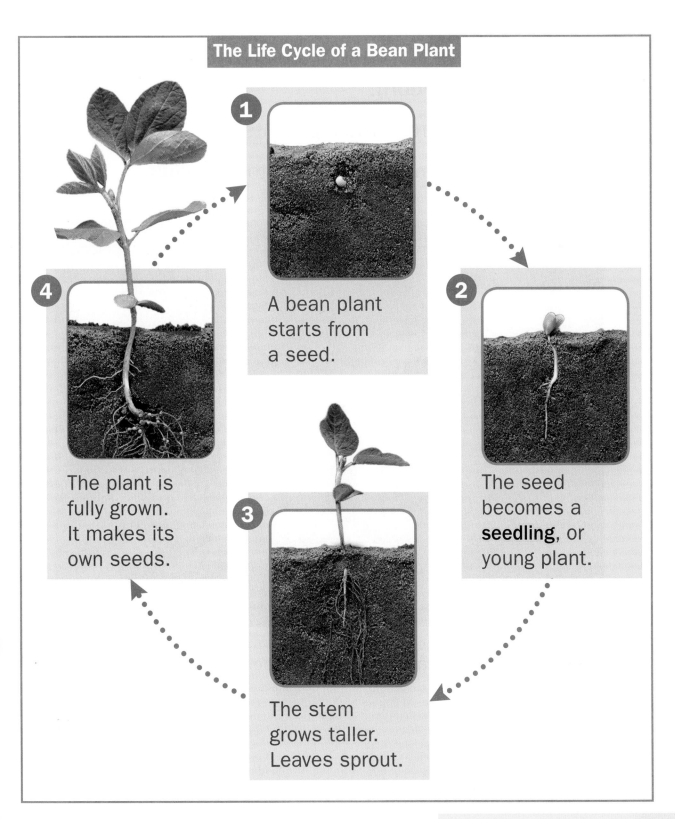

1 A bean plant starts from a seed.

2 The seed becomes a **seedling**, or young plant.

3 The stem grows taller. Leaves sprout.

4 The plant is fully grown. It makes its own seeds.

Animals

Animals are **born**.

They come from their parents.

A young animal **develops** into an **adult**.

tiger

adult

▲ Many baby animals look like their parents.

The Life Cycle of a Sea Turtle

1 The sea turtle goes to land to lay eggs.

4 The sea turtles grow up.

2 The eggs **hatch.**

3 The baby turtles go into the ocean.

WHY IT MATTERS

You go through a life cycle.

Earth Science

Rocks and Minerals

ESSENTIAL IDEA

Rocks are useful. They come from nature.

The Earth has many kinds of **rocks**. Rocks are formed in **nature**.

rocks

Rocks are made of **minerals**. Minerals can be made into things people use.

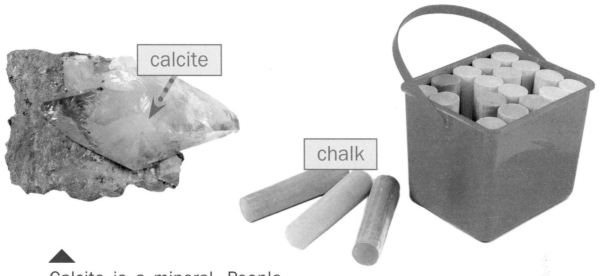

calcite

chalk

▲ Calcite is a mineral. People use calcite to make chalk.

WHY IT MATTERS

You see rocks in roads and buildings. You can wear minerals like gold or silver as jewelry.

Soil

Soil is made up of clay, sand, and humus.

- **Clay** is tiny pieces of mud and rock. It is sticky when wet.

- **Sand** is small pieces of rock. It feels rough.

grass

soil

Humus is made of dead plants and animals.

Soil can have different amounts of clay, sand, humus, air, and water.

▲ This soil has a lot of clay.

▲ This soil has a lot of humus.

WHY IT MATTERS

You can feel the clay in soil.

How Earth Changes

ESSENTIAL IDEA

Earth changes all the time.
The shape of the land changes.

Weathering and erosion change the shape of the land.

The Grand Canyon was formed by weathering and erosion.
▼

Weathering

Sun, wind, and water cause **weathering**.
Weathering changes rocks.

Rain beats on rocks.

Waves pound on rocks.

Erosion

Wind and water cause **erosion**.
Erosion moves rocks, sand, and soil.

Wind throws sand.

Water carries soil.

WHY IT MATTERS

The cracks you see in the street are
caused by weathering.

Fossils

Fossils help us learn about animals and plants from long ago.

Fossils are usually **molds** of a plant or animal.

▲
Fossils help us know how dinosaurs looked long ago.

These footprints in the mud turned into rock.

This fossil shows the shape of a bird.

This is a fossil of a plant.

WHY IT MATTERS

You can learn about animals and plants from long ago from fossils.

Landforms

ESSENTIAL IDEA

Land on Earth has different shapes.

Earth has mountains, hills, plains, and valleys. These are called **landforms**.

A **mountain** is the highest landform.

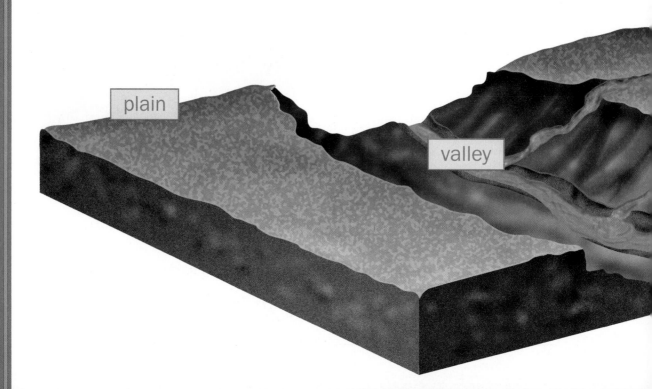

plain

valley

A **hill** is high and rounded at the top.

A **plain** is an area of flat land.

A **valley** is a low area between two higher landforms.

┌─ **WHY IT MATTERS** ─────────

> You live on a landform.

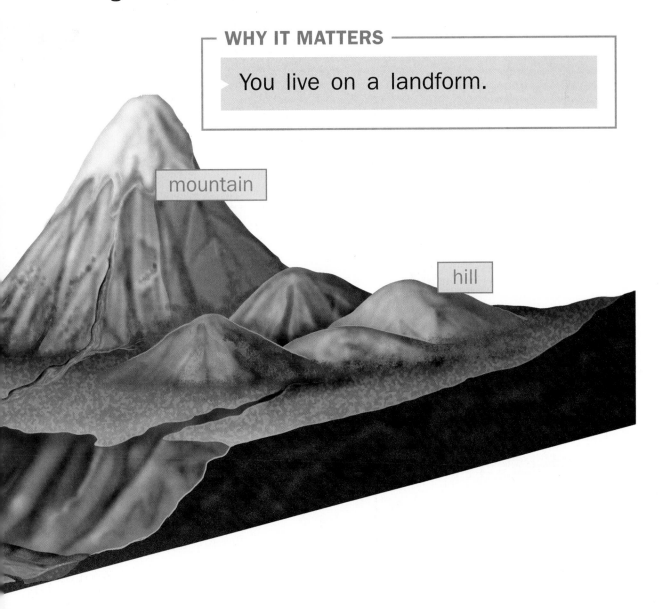

mountain

hill

Water

> Most of Earth's surface is covered with salt water or freshwater.

Salt Water

Oceans cover most of Earth.

An **ocean** is a large body of **salt water**.

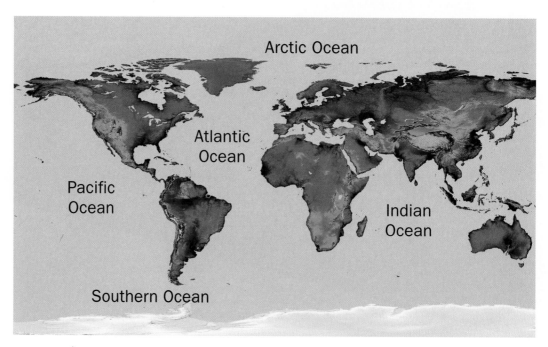

There are five oceans that cover Earth.

Freshwater

Freshwater comes from lakes, rivers, and streams.

A **lake** is water with land all around it.

A **river** has water that moves.

Streams are smaller rivers.

river

◀ A boy is fishing in a river.

WHY IT MATTERS

You drink freshwater.

Pollution

┌─ **ESSENTIAL IDEA** ─────────────────

Pollution is harmful to Earth.

└─────────────────────────────────────

Pollution causes **harm** to land, air, and water. It also harms plants and animals.

This bird is covered in oil. Oil pollutes the water where the bird lives.

▼

Some people throw trash on the ground. Trash pollutes the land and water.

Cars can cause air pollution.

Some factories dump waste into rivers. Waste pollutes the land and water.

WHY IT MATTERS

You can help stop pollution.

Recycling

ESSENTIAL IDEA

People need to reduce, reuse, and recycle to save Earth.

People need to be careful and make less **waste**. Here are three ways to make less waste.

● **Reduce** means to use less.

This boy draws on both sides of a paper. He uses less paper.

Reuse means to use something again.

This jar held jelly. Now it is being reused to hold paint brushes.

Recycle means to change something to use it again.

This girl recycles a drink can. The can will be made into something else.

WHY IT MATTERS

You can help save Earth.
You can reduce, reuse, and recycle.

The Sun and Stars

ESSENTIAL IDEA

The Sun and stars are made of hot gas that glows.

The **Sun** is a star. It is the closest star to Earth. The Sun gives heat and light to living things on Earth.

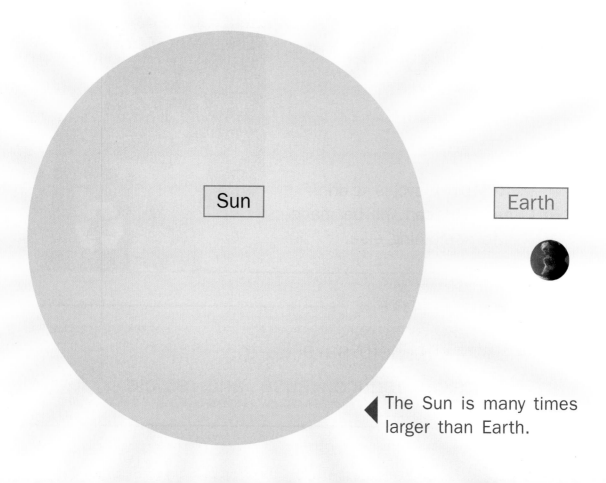

Sun

Earth

The Sun is many times larger than Earth.

stars

▲ You can see stars shine in the sky at night.

A **star** gives off its own light. Stars are balls of very hot glowing gas.

WHY IT MATTERS

> You can see the Sun in the daytime sky.
> You can see stars in the nighttime sky.

Day and Night

ESSENTIAL IDEA

Day and night happen because Earth rotates.

During the day, you see the Sun.
At night you usually see the **Moon**.

Moon

day   night

Earth **rotates**, or spins.

It is day when we face the Sun. When our side turns away from the Sun, night comes.

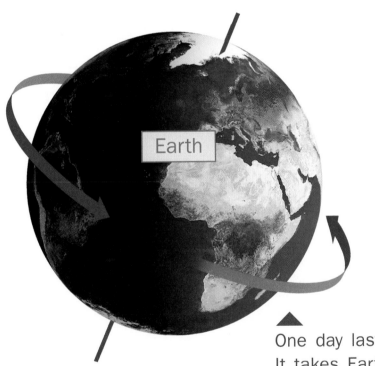

Sun

Earth

One day lasts 24 hours. It takes Earth that long to spin around once.

WHY IT MATTERS

You face away from the Sun at night.
You face the Sun by day.

The Seasons

Seasons happen because Earth tilts toward or away from the Sun.

Earth **revolves**, or moves, around the Sun. It takes one year, or 365 days, for Earth to go around the Sun once.

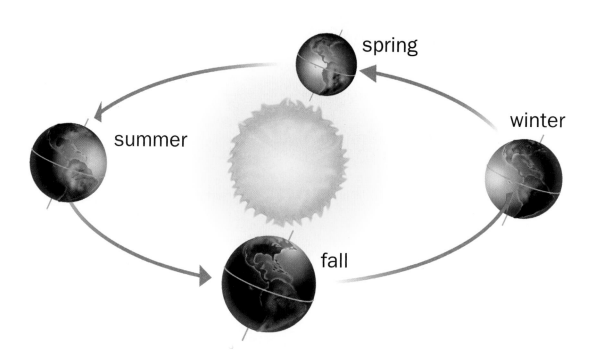

Part of the year, Earth **tilts** toward the Sun. Other times, it tilts away from the Sun. This causes the **seasons**.

spring

winter

summer

fall

WHY IT MATTERS

You do different things in different seasons.

The Solar System

Earth and other planets orbit the Sun.

The Sun is the center of our **solar system**. Planets **orbit**, or go around, the Sun.

Earth Earth is the only planet with human life.

Sun

Venus

Mercury

Mars

Scientists say there are eight main
planets in the solar system.

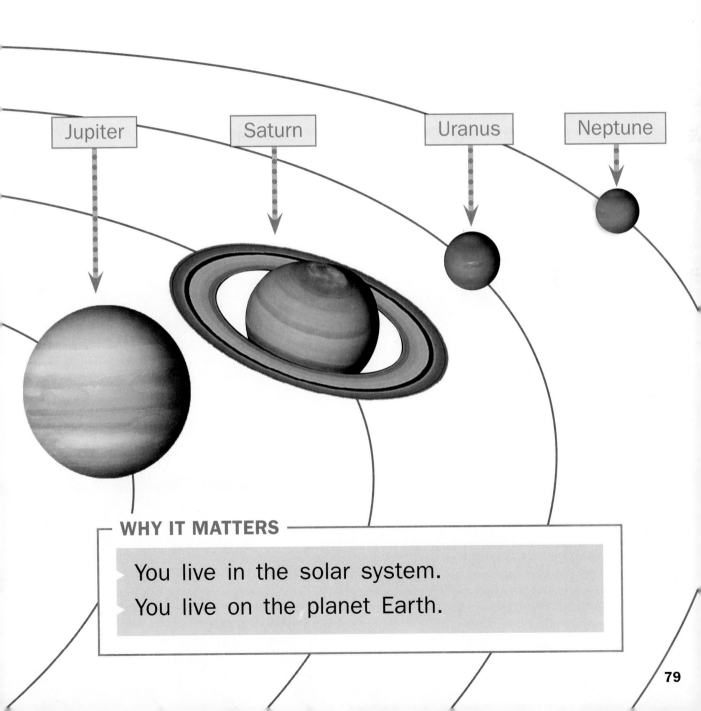

Jupiter   Saturn   Uranus   Neptune

WHY IT MATTERS

> You live in the solar system.
> You live on the planet Earth.

Weather

┌─ **ESSENTIAL IDEA** ─────────────────────┐

There are different kinds of weather.
└──┘

The **weather** is what it is like outside. There may be **clouds** in the sky. Clouds can bring certain kinds of weather.

It is sunny when there are not many clouds.
▼

Sun

sky

cloud

Rain is water that falls from clouds.

Snow is made of ice. It falls from clouds.

Wind is air that moves.

Fog is a cloud near the ground.

WHY IT MATTERS

You can check the weather.
You can dress for the weather.

Measuring the Weather

┌─ **ESSENTIAL IDEA** ─────────────────────┐
│ **Tools help us measure the weather.** │
└───┘

We use tools to measure the weather.

A **thermometer** measures the temperature. The **temperature** tells how hot or cold it is outside.

thermometer

A **rain gauge** measures rain.

rain gauge

A **weather vane** tells the direction of the wind.

weather vane

WHY IT MATTERS

You wear different clothes for different temperatures.

The Water Cycle

ESSENTIAL IDEA

Earth's water goes through a cycle.

Earth's water is always moving between the air and the ground. This movement is called the **water cycle**.

1 The Sun warms up water on Earth. The water changes into **vapor**.

WHY IT MATTERS

The water you drink is part of the water cycle.

2 The vapor rises and changes into tiny water drops. The water drops make clouds.

3 The drops fall from the sky as rain or snow. Rain and snow are types of **precipitation**.

4 The water flows into rivers, lakes, and oceans.

Storms

ESSENTIAL IDEA

Storms are bad weather. There are different kinds of storms.

Thunderstorms

A lot of rain falls during a **thunderstorm**.

There is often a flash of light, or **lightning**. Then you may hear a loud sound called **thunder**.

lightning

You see lightning. Then you hear thunder.

Hurricanes

Hurricanes are strong ocean storms.
They make a lot of rain and strong winds.

ocean

▲
The winds of a hurricane are very strong.

Tornadoes

Tornadoes are strong windstorms that spin.

The winds move across the land. They **destroy** things in their path.

tornado

Blizzards

Blizzards are snowstorms. The wind blows hard and a lot of snow falls.

▲ Roads might close down after a blizzard.

WHY IT MATTERS

> Storms happen everywhere.
> You should protect yourself during a storm.

Physical Science

Matter

┌─ **ESSENTIAL IDEA** ─────────────────────┐

All things are made of matter.

└──┘

Matter is anything that takes up **space**.
All living and nonliving things are matter.

The ground, the ball, and the people are matter.
▼

ball

teacher

student

ground

You can group things by how they look or act. You can group things by their **properties**.

Properties of Matter

Mass is a property. Mass is the amount of matter in something.

less mass (light)	more mass (heavy)
 feather / hat	 elephant / car

WHY IT MATTERS

You and everything around you is matter.

States of Matter

ESSENTIAL IDEA

Matter can be in three states.

Matter can be a solid, liquid, or gas.
All matter takes up space.

gas Air is a gas.

solid A spoon is a solid.

liquid Soup is a liquid.

Solids

Solids take up space. Solids keep their **shape**.

Solids do not change shape if you move them to a new spot.

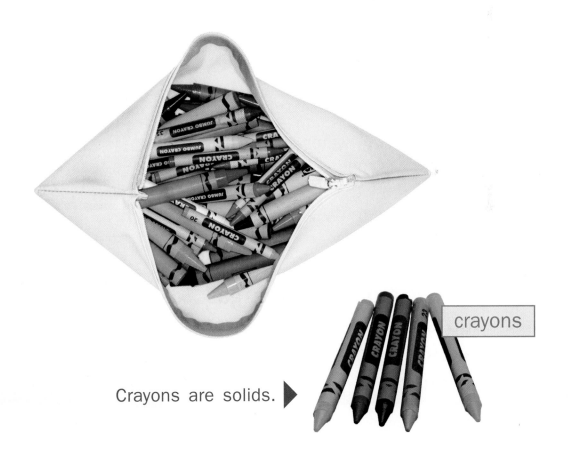

crayons

Crayons are solids. ▶

PHYSICAL SCIENCE

Liquids

Liquids are matter. They take up space. Liquids can **flow**, or move.

water

The water changes its shape to fill the glass. ▶

Gases

The air around you is **gas**. You can't see it, but air takes up space. Gas has no shape.

steam

Steam is a gas. It spreads ▶ out into the air.

States of Matter

Solids keep their shape.

Liquids take the shape of their containers.

Gases spread out to fill their containers.

WHY IT MATTERS

▷ Your pencil is a solid.

▷ The water you drink is a liquid.

▷ The air you breathe is a gas.

PHYSICAL SCIENCE

Changing Matter

ESSENTIAL IDEA

Heating and cooling can change matter.

Matter can change. Water can **freeze** and become a solid. Ice can **melt** and become a liquid.

freeze

▲ Cooling water makes it freeze into ice.

ice

melt water

▲ Heating ice makes it melt into water again.

Water **boils** when it gets very hot. The water changes to a gas called **steam**.

boil

How Matter Changes

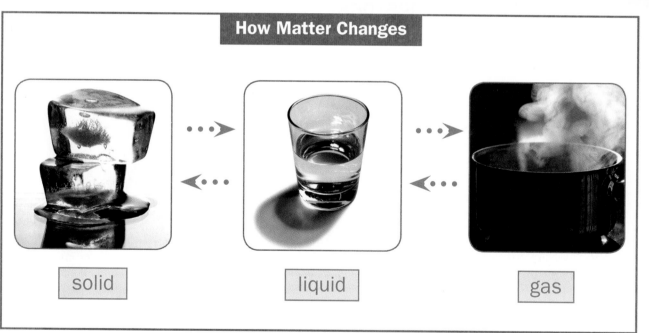

solid   liquid   gas

WHY IT MATTERS

You freeze water to make ice cubes.

Energy

ESSENTIAL IDEA

Energy helps things do work.

Energy makes things work.
It makes things change.

All living things need energy.

Your body uses energy
to play sports. ▶

◀ People use the
energy from an
oven to cook
food.

Earth gets energy from the Sun. Sun energy is called **solar** energy. Energy can come from many **sources**.

Sources of Energy

Sun

food

electricity

battery

WHY IT MATTERS

> You eat food to get energy.
> Many things in your home use energy.

Heat

Heat is a form of energy. It makes things warmer. Sunlight gives off heat. Fire gives off heat, too.

candle

fire

Sun

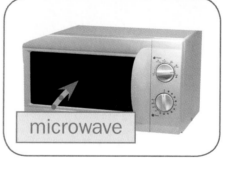

microwave

▲
The energy from all of these things gives off heat.

How Heat Moves

Metal **conducts** heat. This means heat can move through **metal**.

metal

pan

Heat from the stove cooks the food in the pan.

WHY IT MATTERS

You feel heat from the Sun.
Heat is used to cook your food.

Light

ESSENTIAL IDEA

Light helps us see.

Light is a kind of energy. Light comes from many sources.

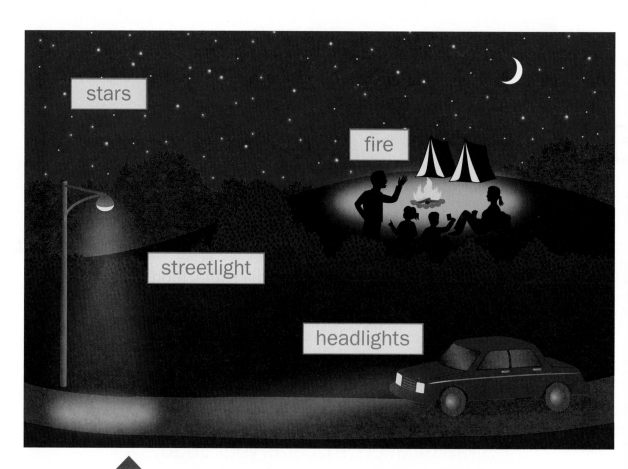

Stars, lights, and fire are all light sources.

Light moves in special ways.

Light moves in straight lines.

Light goes through glass.

glass

Light **reflects** off a mirror.

mirror

Blocked light makes a **shadow**.

shadow

WHY IT MATTERS

Light from the Sun helps you see in daytime.

You turn on the light to see at night.

Sound

ESSENTIAL IDEA

Sound is noise caused by vibrations.

Music, horns, and voices are **sounds**. Sounds are caused by **vibrations**.

The strings on the guitar vibrate to make sound. ▼

strings

guitar

Volume tells how soft or loud a sound is.

soft	loud
a lullaby	a vacuum cleaner

Pitch tells how high or low a sound is.

low	high
a tuba	a bell

WHY IT MATTERS

You make sound when you speak.

Motion

ESSENTIAL IDEA

If something is in motion, it moves.

Things can move from one place to another. Scientists call this **motion**.

▲
The merry-go-round is in motion.

Objects can move fast or slowly. They move at different **speeds**.

Ways Objects Move

Things move in different ways, or **paths**.

straight path

curved path

zigzag path

WHY IT MATTERS

You are in motion when you walk or run.
You can change the path you move in.

Force

Objects can move fast or slow.
move at different speeds.

ESSENTIAL IDEA

A force is a push or pull on something.

You **pull** a wagon. You **push** a shopping cart. The objects move. You move them by using **force**.

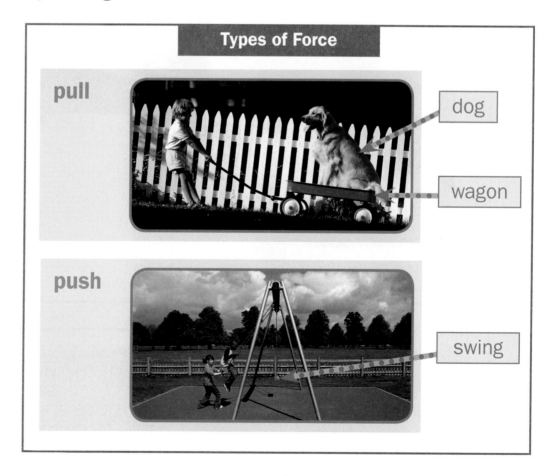

Types of Force

pull

dog

wagon

push

swing

You can change the **amount** of force.

▲ This man uses a lot of force to push the cart.

▲ This child uses a little force to push the button.

WHY IT MATTERS

You use force when you pull or push.

Gravity

ESSENTIAL IDEA

Gravity is a strong force. It pulls things toward the center of Earth.

Earth's **gravity** is a strong force. Gravity pulls things **toward** Earth.

gravity

We try to jump to the sky. Gravity pulls us back to Earth.

Effects of Gravity

action	what happens
You throw a ball.	The ball falls to the ground.

action	what happens
You jump.	You are pulled back to Earth.

WHY IT MATTERS

You stay on Earth because of gravity.
When you let go of things, they fall.

Friction

ESSENTIAL IDEA

Friction slows down or stops objects.

Friction is a force that happens when things rub. Friction **slows** down or **stops** objects.

There is friction between the tire and the street.

Amounts of Friction

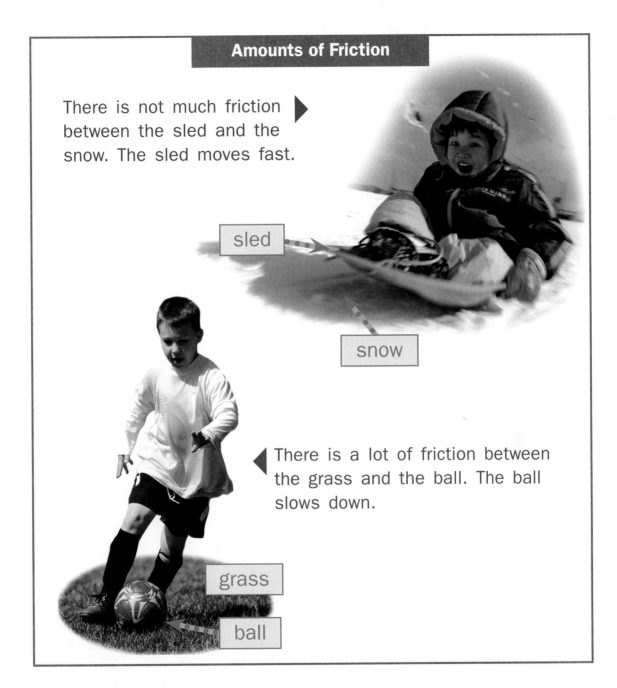

There is not much friction between the sled and the snow. The sled moves fast.

sled

snow

There is a lot of friction between the grass and the ball. The ball slows down.

grass

ball

WHY IT MATTERS

There is friction between your feet and the ground when you walk.

Simple Machines

ESSENTIAL IDEA

Simple machines are tools.
They make work easier to do.

Simple machines help us do **work**.

A **screw** holds things together.

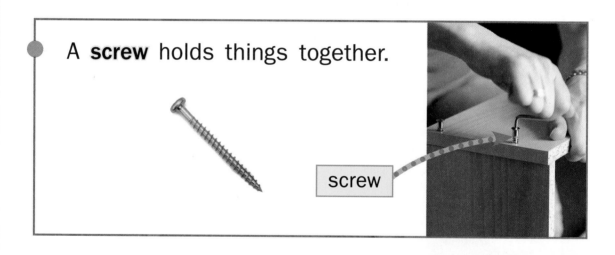

screw

A **pulley** lifts and lowers something.

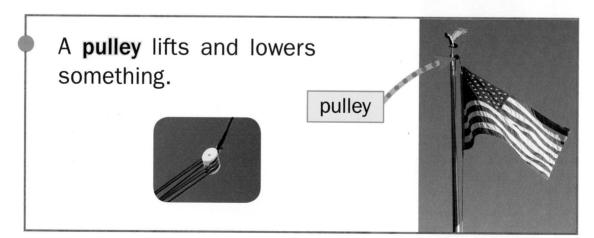

pulley

A **wedge** separates two things.

wedge

A **lever** moves or lifts something.

lever

WHY IT MATTERS

You use simple machines to do work.

You use tools every day.

Magnets

ESSENTIAL IDEA

Magnets attract some objects.

Iron can be made into a **magnet**. Magnets **attract** other things made with iron.

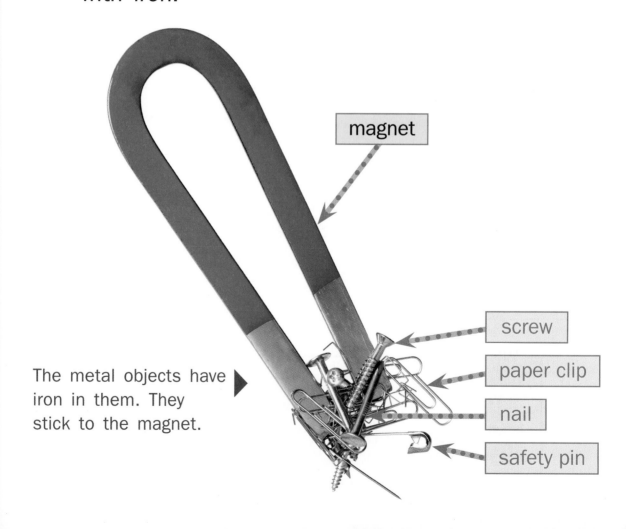

magnet

The metal objects have iron in them. They stick to the magnet.

screw

paper clip

nail

safety pin

Where You See Magnets

Magnets are around us all the time.

refrigerator

crane

magnets

▲ The refrigerator is made of metal. The magnets stick to it.

▲ This crane has a strong magnet. The magnet is used to pick up heavy pieces of metal.

WHY IT MATTERS

You use things with magnets all the time, such as toys and doors.

Technology

ESSENTIAL IDEA

Technology is using what we know to make something new.

Scientists use what they have learned to make new things. These new things are **technology.**

computer

People use technology to make things easier and better.

Where You See Technology

A **computer** is technology. There are many kinds of technology.

computer

microscope

white board

calculator

WHY IT MATTERS

> You use technology at school.

121

 # Studying Science

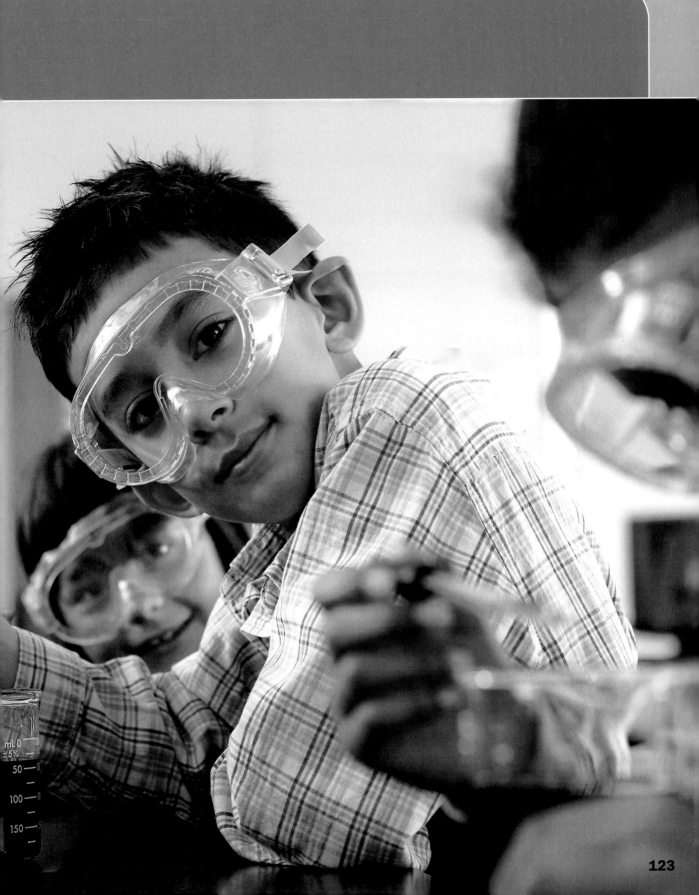

mL 0
±5%
50
100
150

Science Process Skills

ESSENTIAL IDEA

Scientists ask questions. Scientists look for answers.

People who study science are called **scientists**. Scientists ask **questions**.

What do seeds need to grow?

Scientists look for **answers** to their questions. The scientists use these **skills**.

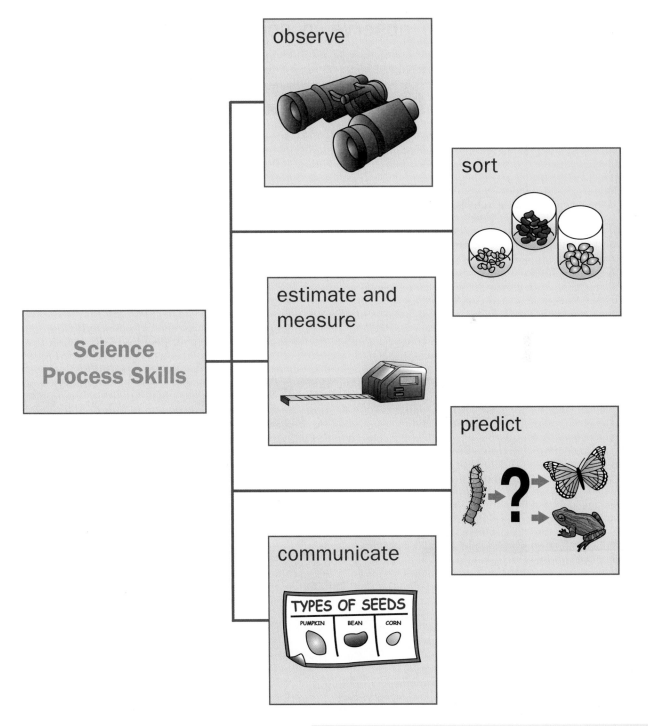

observe

sort

estimate and measure

predict

communicate

TYPES OF SEEDS

PUMPKIN | BEAN | CORN

Science Process Skills

STUDYING SCIENCE

Observe

You have five **senses**. You use your senses to **observe** in science.

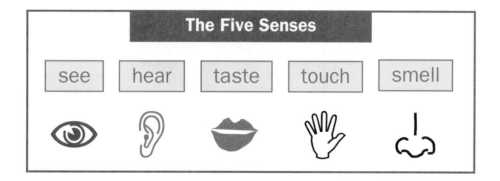

The shell feels bumpy.

shell

126

Sort

You **sort** things into **groups**.

You look for **patterns**. Some things are the same. Some are different.

You can sort by color, shape, and size.

Name _____ Date _____

Sorting Seeds

small	large
dark	light

STUDYING SCIENCE

Estimate and Measure

You might **estimate** how big or small something is. You make a good guess.

I think the pencil is 13 centimeters long.

You **measure** a thing to find out its size or weight.

▲
The pencil is 13 centimeters long.

Predict

You **predict** when you guess what may happen next. Then you check your guess.

cocoon

▲ Predict what you will see in a cocoon.

butterfly

▲ Check your prediction.

Communicate

In science, you **communicate**.
You tell others what you have learned.

You can communicate with **words**
or **pictures**.

▲ This student uses words and pictures
to communicate about the weather.

You can use science process skills in any order. Use these skills to help you answer questions in science.

Science Process Skills	
skill	
observe	
sort	
estimate and measure	
predict	
communicate	

WHY IT MATTERS

You use science process skills to find the answers to questions about science.

Using Science Methods

Scientists use special methods to help them solve problems.

All science starts with a question.

Name _____ Date _____

Science Methods

My Question

Why is it dark at

night?

Scientists use special **methods** to help them answer their questions.

Science Methods

Make a Hypothesis
Collect Data
Make a Conclusion

Make a Hypothesis

Make a guess about the answer to your question. The guess is called a **hypothesis**.

My Hypothesis

I think the Sun turns off at night with a switch.

Collect Data

Next, collect and check **data**, or facts. You can read a book, observe, or do an **experiment**.

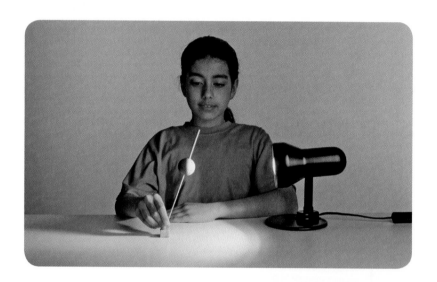

My Data

One part of Earth is dark.
One part is light.
I can spin the Earth to make
light shine where it was dark.

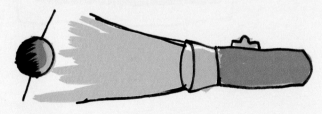

Make a Conclusion

Tell whether your hypothesis was right or wrong. In a **conclusion**, you tell what you learned.

My Conclusion

My hypothesis was wrong.

The Sun does not turn off.

Earth spins.

The Sun side has day.

The other side has night.

WHY IT MATTERS

You use science methods to find answers to science questions.

Part Two

Literacy Essentials

This part of the book will help you read and write about science.

READING SCIENCE 138

The lessons in this section show you how to use text features to help you read.

COMPREHENSION 154

These lessons teach you strategies and skills for reading.

UNDERSTANDING LANGUAGE 176

This section helps you learn phrases and words in the English language.

WRITING FOR SCIENCE 182

The lessons in this section show you how to write a science report.

Reading Science

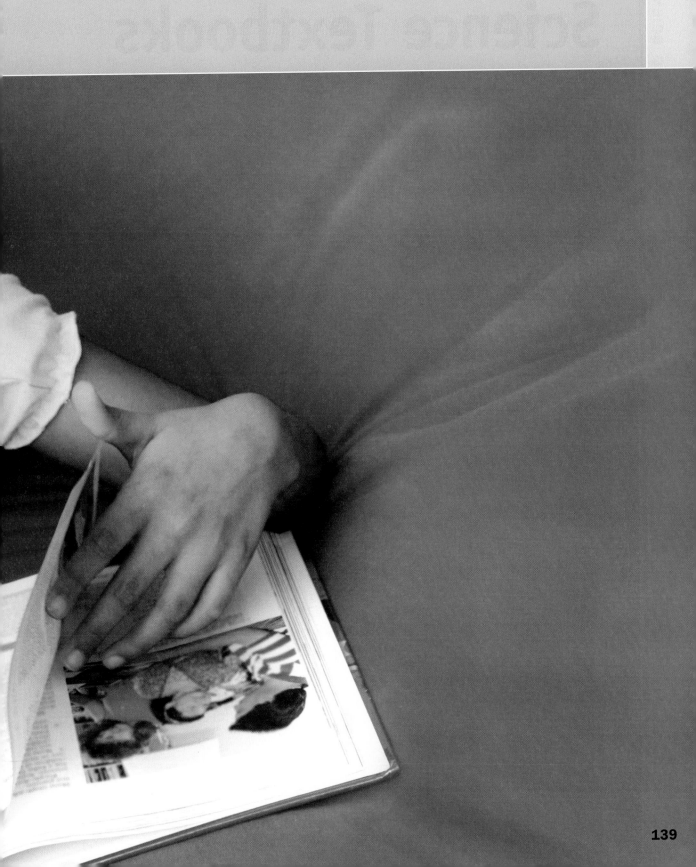

Science Textbooks

ESSENTIAL IDEA

Science textbooks help you learn science.

A **textbook** is a book to help you. It is **organized** by **topic**.

Units name big topics. **Chapters** tell about smaller topics in each unit.

UNIT 1 **Life Science**

Chapter 1

Chapter 2

Chapter 3

Chapter 1 **Plants**

You read textbooks for a reason, or with a **purpose**.

Read with a Purpose

1 Ask yourself what you want to learn.

2 Find a chapter about that topic.

3 Read the chapter.

I want to learn about plants. I will read Chapter 1, "Plants."

WHY IT MATTERS

You use science textbooks to learn information.

Magazines and Newspapers

ESSENTIAL IDEA

Magazines and newspapers can give facts about science.

Stories in magazines and newspapers are called **articles**. Articles have **headlines** and **pictures**.

NATION

Hurricane Comes to Texas

headline

picture

HOUSTON: A hurricane named Humberto passed through Texas last week. The hurricane caused heavy rain and strong winds. Many homes lost electricity.

Hurricane Humberto brought heavy rain and winds.

How to Preview

Before you read, **preview** the article.

1 Read the headline.

2 Look at any pictures.

3 Think about what you will read.

I think this article will be about a hurricane that came to Texas.

WHY IT MATTERS

You can read articles to learn new ideas and facts about a topic.

Internet

ESSENTIAL IDEA

The Internet is a fast way to get information.

You can **search** for science facts on the **Internet**.

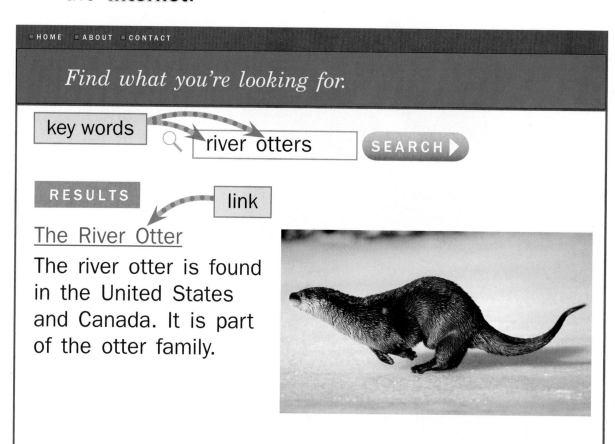

How to Search the Internet

1 Think about **key words** for your topic. Type your key words into the search box.

2 Read the results. Choose the best **Web site**.

3 Click on the **link** of that Web site.

WHY IT MATTERS

You use the Internet to look for information.

Parts of a Textbook

ESSENTIAL IDEA

A textbook has parts that help you find information.

Textbooks have parts to help you find information faster.

table of contents The table of contents is in the front of a textbook.

glossary The glossary is in the back.

index The index is in the back too.

Table of Contents

The **table of contents** tells you on what page the **units** and **chapters** start.

Contents

Contents

HOW TO USE THIS BOOK **10**

Previewing Lessons 12
Learning Academic Vocabulary 13

unit

chapter

Part One Science Essentials **14**

LIFE SCIENCE **16**

Living Things 18
What Plants Need 20
Parts of a Plant 22
Kinds of Plants 24
How Plants Are Adapted 26
Habitats 28
Types of Animals 34
How Animals Are Adapted 42
Endangered Animals 44
Food Energy 46
The Food Chain 48
Life Cycles 50

5

The chapter "What Plants Need" starts on page 20.

READING SCIENCE

Glossary

A **glossary** gives the meaning, or **definition**, of special words in the book.

glossary

GLOSSARY

Glossary

definition

A

adapt (ə dăpt′) *v.* change to better fit the environment, **26, 42**

adult (ə dŭlt′ *or* ăd′ŭlt) *n.* a living thing that is fully grown, **52**

alike (ə līk′) *adj.* the same as something else, **156**

alphabetical order (ăl′fə bĕt′ĭ kəl ôr′dər) *n.* when a list is set up in the order of the alphabet, **149**

amount (ə mount′) *n.* level or quantity; how much of something, **111**

balance (băl′əns) *n.* a tool that is used to compare the mass of two things, **193**

birds (bûrdz) *n.* warm-blooded animals with backbones that have wings and feathers, **36**

blizzards (blĭz′ərdz) *n.* winter storms with heavy winds and a lot of snow, **89**

boil (boil) *v.* become very hot and change from a liquid into a gas, **99**

born (bôrn) *v.* become alive or begin life, **52**

breathe (brēth) *v.* move air in and out of a body, **37**

I'm not sure what *process* means. I can look in the glossary to find out!

Index

The **index** gives all the topics in a book in **alphabetical order**.

Page numbers tell you where to find each topic.

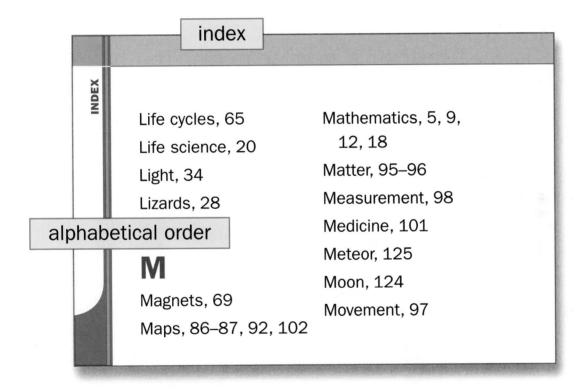

index

Life cycles, 65
Life science, 20
Light, 34
Lizards, 28

alphabetical order

M

Magnets, 69
Maps, 86–87, 92, 102

Mathematics, 5, 9, 12, 18
Matter, 95–96
Measurement, 98
Medicine, 101
Meteor, 125
Moon, 124
Movement, 97

WHY IT MATTERS

> You can find information faster if you know the parts of a textbook.

Textbook Features

Textbooks have features that give you more information.

Science textbooks have **features**. The features can help you read.

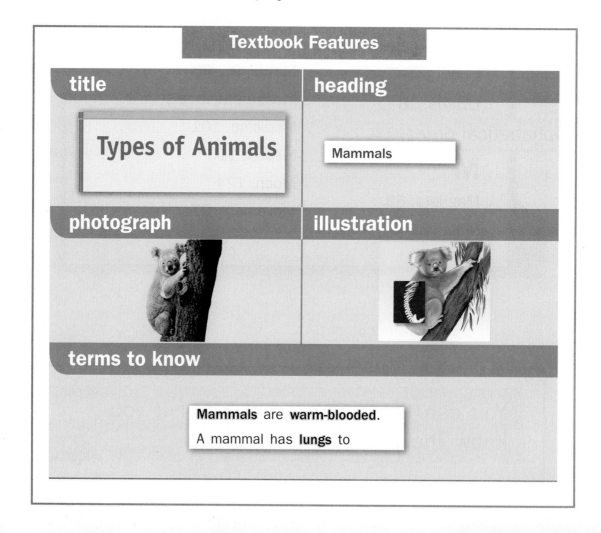

Textbook Features

title	heading
Types of Animals	Mammals
photograph	illustration
terms to know	

Mammals are **warm-blooded**.
A mammal has **lungs** to

Titles and Headings

The **title** tells you the big topic.
The **heading** tells you about a smaller part of that topic.

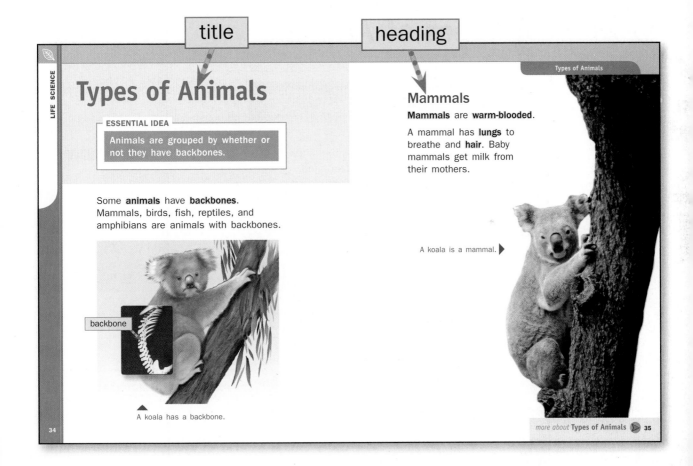

title

heading

LIFE SCIENCE

Types of Animals

ESSENTIAL IDEA

Animals are grouped by whether or not they have backbones.

Some **animals** have **backbones**. Mammals, birds, fish, reptiles, and amphibians are animals with backbones.

backbone

▲ A koala has a backbone.

34

Types of Animals

Mammals

Mammals are **warm-blooded**.

A mammal has **lungs** to breathe and **hair**. Baby mammals get milk from their mothers.

A koala is a mammal. ▶

more about Types of Animals ▷ 35

Terms to Know

Words in dark print are **terms to know**.
These words are important to learn.

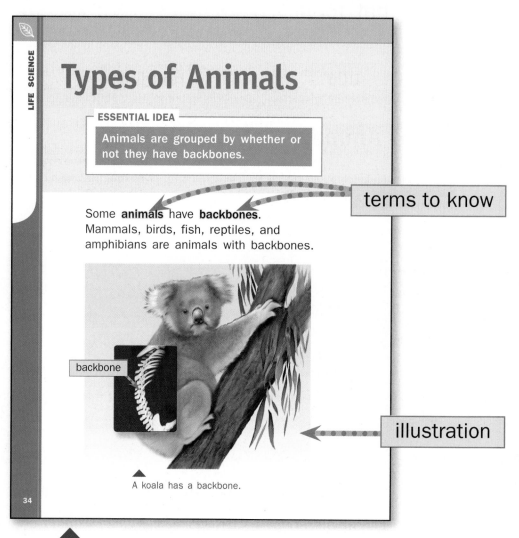

LIFE SCIENCE

Types of Animals

ESSENTIAL IDEA

Animals are grouped by whether or not they have backbones.

Some **animals** have **backbones**.
Mammals, birds, fish, reptiles, and amphibians are animals with backbones.

terms to know

backbone

illustration

▲ A koala has a backbone.

34

▲ Words in bold, dark print are important to remember.

Photographs and Illustrations

Photographs show real people, places, and things. **Illustrations** are drawings.

Captions tell more about the photograph or illustration.

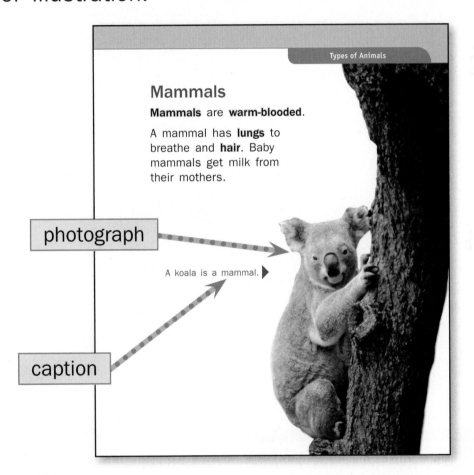

Types of Animals

Mammals

Mammals are **warm-blooded**.

A mammal has **lungs** to breathe and **hair**. Baby mammals get milk from their mothers.

photograph

A koala is a mammal. ▶

caption

WHY IT MATTERS

You use all the features of a textbook to help you read.

Comprehension

Comparing and Contrasting

ESSENTIAL IDEA

Comparing and contrasting shows how things are alike and different.

Compare things to tell how they are **alike**.

Contrast things to tell how they are **different**.

Frogs and Toads

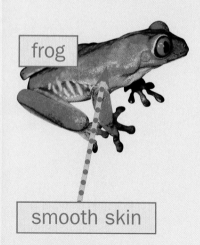

frog

smooth skin

Both frogs and toads live in water when they are young. Frogs have smooth skin, **but** toads have bumpy skin.

toad

bumpy skin

Organize your ideas to compare and contrast.

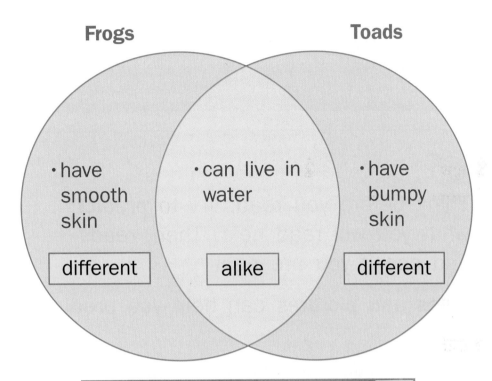

Frogs **Toads**

- have smooth skin

- can live in water

- have bumpy skin

| different | alike | different |

Compare and Contrast Words	
compare	**contrast**
both	but
too	however
also	unlike

WHY IT MATTERS

> You can tell how you and your friends are alike and different.

Predicting

ESSENTIAL IDEA

Good readers think about what might happen next.

Think before you read. Try to **predict** what you will read next. Then, read and see if you are right.

Titles and **pictures** can help you predict.

Riding Trains [title]

Have you ever been on a train? People ride trains every day. Trains go on train tracks.

[picture]

How to Predict

1 Look at the title.

2 Look at the picture.

3 Predict what you will read next.

I think this article will be about trains.

WHY IT MATTERS

You predict to help you think about what you will read.

Determining Important Information

The most important part of what you read is called the **main idea**.

Details tell facts about the main idea.

The Red-Eyed Tree Frog

The red-eyed tree frog is a rain forest animal. — main idea

The red-eyed tree frog has red eyes. It has a green body. Its feet are orange. — details

Finding What Is Important

You can list details to help you find the main idea.

Main Idea

The red-eyed tree frog is a rain forest animal.

Detail

The red-eyed tree frog has red eyes.

Detail

It has a green body.

WHY IT MATTERS

The main idea tells you what is most important.

Summarizing

A **summary** tells only about important ideas.

You can **summarize** ideas. You tell or write about the ideas in your own words.

FOSSILS

A fossil shows life from long ago. ← main idea

A fossil is made from a plant or an animal. ← important fact

A fossil might show bones. An old footprint can be a fossil. Scientists learn lots of things from fossils.

How to Summarize

1 Read the text.

2 Tell the main idea and important facts in your own words.

3 Leave out the small details.

Topic: __Fossils__

Fossils tell scientists about life from long ago. Fossils are formed from animals and plants.

summary

WHY IT MATTERS

Summarizing helps you understand what you read.

Making Inferences

ESSENTIAL IDEA

Good readers ask what information might be missing. Then they guess what it is.

When you read, sometimes you need to make an **inference**. You make a good guess to help you understand.

flowers

bird

Spring

Spring is a new beginning. Trees get new leaves. Flowers bloom. Eggs hatch. Birds chirp. Animal babies are born.

How to Make an Inference

Use what you know and what you read to make an inference.

1 What does the story say?

New things grow in spring.

2 What do you know that the story does not say?

Spring is warmer than winter.

3 Put the information together to make an inference.

Warm weather must help new things grow.

inference

WHY IT MATTERS

You add meaning when you make an inference, or guess.

Visualizing

┌─ **ESSENTIAL IDEA** ─────────────────

Good readers visualize. They see pictures in their head as they read.

As you read, **visualize**. Make pictures in your **mind** to help you understand the text.

The Bear Gets Ready for Winter

It is almost winter in the mountains. The bear looks for a winter den. A den is a warm place to sleep during the winter. Caves make good dens for bears.

How to Visualize

1 Read the text.

2 Think about something in the text. What does it look like?

3 Make a picture in your mind.

cave

WHY IT MATTERS

You visualize to make sense of what you read.

Asking and Answering Questions

Take time to **pause**, or stop, when you read. Ask yourself **questions**. Get **answers** before you go on.

Light Shines on Us All

Light is part of our lives. We see the Sun in the morning. We use lamps, candles, and flashlights at night.

The Sun is our most important light source. The Sun is far away, but it is very bright.

Sun

Ask and Answer Questions

Asking and answering questions helps you understand what you read.

question

What are some light sources?

answer

We get light from the Sun, lamps, candles, and flashlights.

WHY IT MATTERS

You ask and answer questions to make sense of what you read.

Monitoring Comprehension

ESSENTIAL IDEA

Good readers check comprehension. They use fix-up tips.

The word **monitor** means "check." Good readers check that they **understand** what they read.

Plant Adaptations

Plants have adapted to stay safe. Some plants have spines. Some plants taste bad. Some plants make animals itch.

These adaptations make it hard for animals to eat them.

spines

Fix-up Tips

Use **fix-up** tips to help you understand.

1 Go back and reread.

2 Read on. See if the answer comes to you.

3 Ask for help.

Adapted is a new word for me.

Use one of the fix-up tips. You could reread.

WHY IT MATTERS

You understand better when you check as you read.

Identifying Cause-Effect

ESSENTIAL IDEA

Good readers figure out why things happen.

A **cause** is what makes something happen.

An **effect** is what happens.

The Daily News

Tornado Hits Oklahoma

Last month, a tornado hit Oklahoma. The tornado caused a lot of damage. The tornado broke trees. It also broke the roofs and windows of buildings.

cause

effect

tornado

The tornado is the cause of damage. The effect is damaged trees and buildings.

WHY IT MATTERS

You read to learn why things happen.

Making Connections

ESSENTIAL IDEA

Good readers make connections as they read.

Sometimes you make a **connection** when you read. What you read relates to something in your own life.

Cats and Fur

Like all mammals, cats have fur. Cats get rid of their extra fur in warm weather. Cats shed their fur so they don't get too hot.

If you have a pet cat, you may find fur on chairs, beds, and clothes.

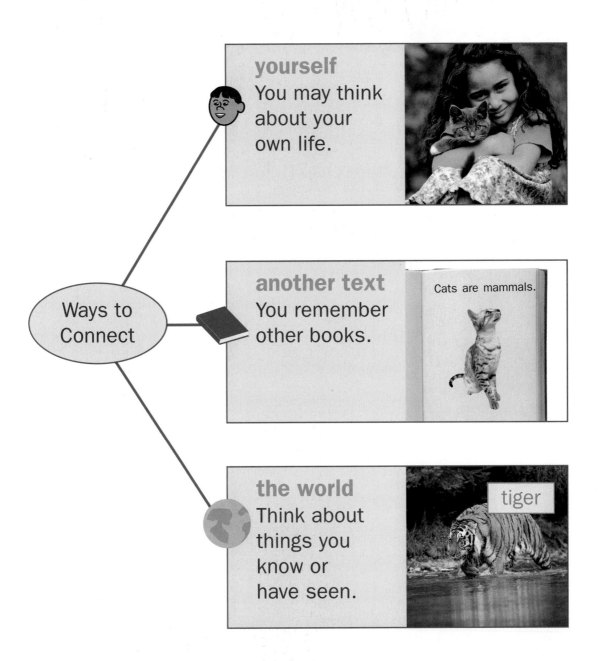

yourself
You may think about your own life.

another text
You remember other books.

Cats are mammals.

the world
Think about things you know or have seen.

tiger

Ways to Connect

WHY IT MATTERS

You make connections to what you read.
Making connections helps you remember.

Understanding Language

Prefixes and Suffixes

┌─ **ESSENTIAL IDEA** ─────────────┐

Prefixes and suffixes change the
meaning of words.

└──────────────────────────────────┘

A **prefix** is a group of letters at the start
of a word.

bi + **cycle** = **bicycle**

↑
prefix

A **suffix** is a group of letters at the end
of a word.

color + **ful** = **colorful**

↑
suffix

Prefix Examples

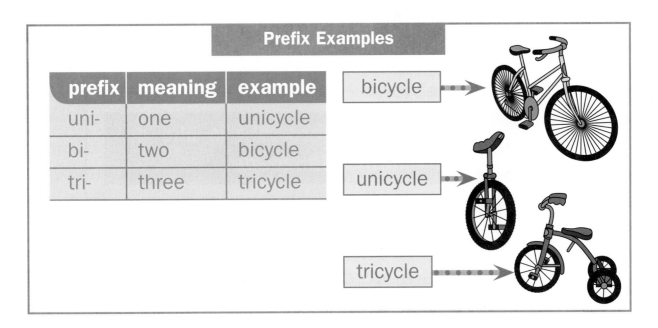

prefix	meaning	example
uni-	one	unicycle
bi-	two	bicycle
tri-	three	tricycle

bicycle

unicycle

tricycle

Suffix Examples

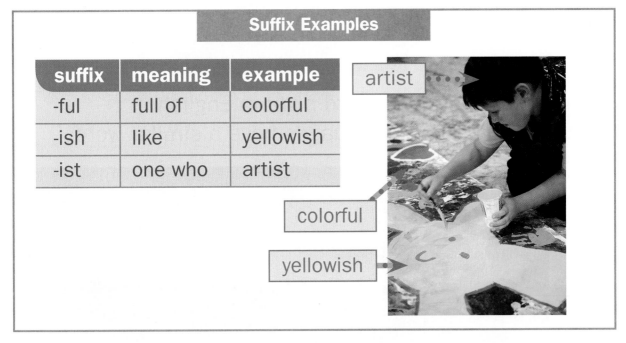

suffix	meaning	example
-ful	full of	colorful
-ish	like	yellowish
-ist	one who	artist

artist

colorful

yellowish

WHY IT MATTERS

Prefixes and suffixes help you learn more words.

Cognates

Cognates are words in different **languages** that look or sound alike. The words mean the same thing.

Cognates for *Night*

You know the word *night* in English. Some other languages have a **similar** word.

nuit	nacht	nicht	natt
(French)	(German, Dutch)	(Scots)	(Swedish)

English-Spanish Cognates

Many English words have Spanish cognates.

English	Spanish	
flower	flor	
camera	cámara	
circle	círculo	
elephant	elefante	
telephone	teléfono	

WHY IT MATTERS

Cognates can help you learn new words.

Writing for Science

Taking Notes

ESSENTIAL IDEA

Taking notes helps you remember important ideas.

Notes are pieces of information. Notes are a **summary** of important ideas.

Saturn

Saturn is the sixth planet from the Sun. Saturn is very big. Saturn is over 750 times bigger than Earth!

Saturn has rings. The rings are made of rocks and ice. Some chunks of rock and ice are bigger than a truck. Some are small like sand.

How to Take Notes

1 Write important words and ideas.

2 Make notes short.

3 Do not copy whole sentences.

4 Write the **source** of the information.

Topic: <u>Saturn</u> notes

- <u>sixth planet</u>
- <u>bigger than Earth</u>
- <u>rings of rock and ice</u>

Source: <u>Planets book</u>

WHY IT MATTERS

You may use notes to write a report.

Organizing Ideas

ESSENTIAL IDEA

Good writers organize their ideas.

You **organize** your ideas to decide what is most important. You make a plan. The plan is called an **outline**.

outline

clouds

Name _____ Date _____

Topic: _Clouds_____

Main Idea: _Clouds are in_

_the sky._____

1. _different shapes_____

2. _made of water_____

3. _make rain or snow____

How to Organize Ideas

1 Write your **topic** on the top of the page.

2 Write the **main idea**.

3 Write **details** in the order you want to talk about them.

WHY IT MATTERS

An outline can help you get ready to write.

Writing About Ideas

┌─ **ESSENTIAL IDEA** ─────────────────────

Good writers follow steps to write
their ideas.

└───

You took notes. You organized your ideas.
Now you are ready to write a **report**.

Steps to Writing a Report

1 Write a **title** at the top of the page.

2 Put your **main idea** in the first sentence.

3 Give some **details** about the main idea.

4 End your paragraph with a **conclusion**.

---

report

Clouds ← title

Clouds are in the sky. ← main idea

Clouds can be different shapes.
They are made of water
vapor. The water in clouds can
fall down as rain or snow. ← details

Clouds are part of nature. ← conclusion

WHY IT MATTERS

You follow steps to write a report.

Science References

Science Tools

ESSENTIAL IDEA

Scientists use different kinds of tools.

Scientists use **tools** to help answer questions.

- You can use a **ruler** to measure how long something is.

ruler

- You can use a **hand lens** to make objects look larger.

hand lens

You can use a **balance** to compare the mass of two things.

balance

You can use a **stopwatch** or a clock to measure time.

stopwatch

WHY IT MATTERS

You may use science tools when you do an experiment.

Science Safety

ESSENTIAL IDEA

You need to be careful in science class.

Here are five safety rules to remember.

1 Follow your teacher's **instructions** carefully.

2 Always protect your eyes by wearing **goggles**.

3 Put **materials** and tools away when you finish an experiment.

4 Work with your teacher to clean up any **spills** right away.

5 **Wash** your hands when you are done.

WHY IT MATTERS

Following safety rules can keep you from getting hurt.

Glossary

A

adapt (ə dăpt′) v. change to better fit the environment, **26, 42**

adult (ə dŭlt′ *or* ăd′ŭlt) n. a living thing that is fully grown, **52**

alike (ə līk′) adj. the same as something else, **156**

alphabetical order (ăl′fə bĕt′ĭ kəl ôr′dər) n. when a list is set up in the order of the alphabet, **149**

amount (ə mount′) n. level or quantity; how much of something, **111**

amphibians (ăm fĭb′ē ənz) n. animals with a backbone that are usually born in water and live on land as adults, **39**

animals (ăn′ə məlz) n. living things, such as dogs and cats, **18, 34**

answers (an′sərz) n. responses to questions, **125, 168**

articles (är′tĭ kəlz) n. stories in magazines and newspapers, **142**

attract (ə trăkt′) v. pull together, **118**

B

backbones (băk′bōnz′) n. the bones in the backs of some animals, **34, 40**

balance (băl′əns) n. a tool that is used to compare the mass of two things, **193**

birds (bûrdz) n. warm-blooded animals with backbones that have wings and feathers, **36**

blizzards (blĭz′ərdz) n. winter storms with heavy winds and a lot of snow, **89**

boil (boil) v. become very hot and change from a liquid into a gas, **99**

born (bôrn) v. become alive or begin life, **52**

breathe (brēth) v. move air in and out of a body, **37**

C

captions (kăp′shənz) n. words that describe a photograph or illustration, **153**

carnivores (kär′nə vôrz′ *or* kär′nə vōrz′) n. animals that eat only meat, **47**

cause (kôz) n. what makes something happen, **172**

chapters (chăp′tərz) n. parts of textbooks that give information about each unit, **140, 147**

clay (klā) n. tiny pieces of rock that are smooth, soft, and sticky when wet, **58**

clouds (kloudz) *n.* collections of water droplets in the sky that can cause rain, snow, or fog, **80**

cognates (kŏg′nāts′) *n.* words in different languages that look and sound alike, **180**

cold-blooded (kōld′ blŭd′ĭd) *adj.* having a body temperature that changes when the outside temperature changes, **38**

communicate (kə myo͞o′nĭ kāt′) *v.* share information with other people, **130**

compare (kəm pâr′) *v.* tell how things are alike, **156**

computer (kəm pyo͞o′tər) *n.* a tool that makes some types of work easier, **120**

conclusion (kən klo͞o′zhən) *n.* the end idea; when you put information together to say what you know, **135, 188**

conduct (kən dŭkt′) *v.* let heat move from one material to another, **103**

cones (kōnz) *n.* the round or long bunches of wood that hold the seeds of some plants, **25**

connection (kə nĕkt′shən) *n.* how one thing connects or relates to another thing, **174**

consumers (kən so͞o′mərz) *n.* living things that must eat other living things to get energy, **46**

contrast (kən trăst′ *or* kŏn′trăst′) *v.* tell how things are different, **156**

Glossary

Pronunciation Key

ă	bat	ô	all
ā	ape	oi	toy
âr	**air**	ou	sh**ou**t
ä	father	o͝o	book
ĕ	let	o͞o	moon
ē	**ea**sy	ŭ	nut
ĭ	if	ûr	circle
ī	lie	ə	ago
îr	d**ear**	ər	moth**er**
ŏ	lot	′	primary stress
ō	go	′	secondary stress

D

data (dā′tə *or* dăt′ə *or* dä′tə) *n.* facts or information, **134**

definition (dĕf′ə nĭsh′ən) *n.* the meaning of a word, **148**

desert (dĕz′ərt) *n.* a dry habitat that gets little rain, **30**

destroy (dĭ stroi′) *v.* break something so it cannot be used anymore, **88**

details (dĭ tālz′ *or* dē′tālz′) *n.* small ideas that support the main idea, **160, 187, 188**

develop (dĭ vĕl′əp) *v.* become or turn into, **52**

different (dĭf′ər ənt *or* dĭf′rənt) *adj.* not the same as something else, **156**

E

effect (ĭ fĕkt′) *n.* what happens, **172**

endangered (ĕn dān′jərd) *adj.* showing signs or warnings that a living thing is in danger of not surviving, **44**

energy (ĕn′ər jē) *n.* what is needed to make things move or do work, **21**, **100**

environment (ĕn vī′rən mənt *or* ĕn vī′ərn mənt) *n.* the area around a living thing, **26**

erosion (ĭ rō′zhən) *n.* process that happens when wind and water carry away loose rocks and soil, **61**

estimate (ĕs′tə māt′) *v.* make your best guess using what you know about the amount of something, **128**

experiment (ĭk spĕr′ə mənt) *n.* a scientific test, **134**

extinct (ĭk stĭngkt′) *adj.* no longer found in nature, **45**

F

feathers (fĕth′ərz) *n.* the soft things that cover the bodies of birds, **36**

features (fē′chərz) *n.* characteristics of something, **42**, **150**

fins (fĭnz) *n.* the parts of a fish that help it swim, **37**

fish (fĭsh) *n.* cold-blooded animals that live in water and have gills, scales, and a backbone, **37**

fix-up (fĭks′ŭp) *adj.* having to do with making something better, **171**

flow (flō) *v.* move, **96**

flowers (flou′ərz) *n.* the parts of some plants that make seeds, **22**, **24**

fog (fôg *or* fŏg) *n.* a cloud near the ground, **81**

food chain (fōōd′ chān) *n.* a diagram that shows what animals eat in a habitat, **48**

force (fôrs *or* fōrs) *n.* a push or pull on something, **110**

forest (fôr′ĭst *or* fōr′ĭst) *n.* a habitat that has many trees, **29**

fossils (fŏs′əlz) *n.* signs of animals and plants from long ago, **62**

freeze (frēz) *v.* become solid, **98**

freshwater (frĕsh′wô′tər *or* frĕsh′wŏt′ər) *n.* water that you can drink, **67**

friction (frĭk′shən) *n.* a force that happens between two things that rub against each other, **114**

fruit (frōōt) *n.* parts of plants that hold seeds, **24**

G

gas (găs) *n.* the state of matter that will fill whatever it is put in, such as steam, **96**

gills (gĭlz) *n.* things that help fish breathe under water, **37**

glossary (glô′sə rē *or* glōs′ə rē) *n.* a part in the back of a book that lists definitions of key words, **148**

goggles (gŏg′əlz) *n.* things you wear to protect your eyes during an experiment, **194**

grassland (grăs′lănd′) *n.* a habitat covered by tall grasses that has few trees, **31**

gravity (grăv′ĭ tē) *n.* a force that pulls objects toward the center of Earth, **112**

groups (gro͞ops) *n.* types or kinds of things that are alike, **127**

H

habitat (hăb′ĭ tăt′) *n.* a place with living and nonliving things; a place where living things make their home, **28**

hair (hâr) *n.* thin strings that grow from a mammal's skin, **35**

hand lens (hănd′ lĕnz′) *n.* a tool that makes things look larger, **193**

harm (härm) *n.* damage or bad things that happen, **68**

hatch (hăch) *v.* break out of an egg, **53**

heading (hĕd′ĭng) *n.* words before text that tell what the text is about, **151**

headlines (hĕd′līnz′) *n.* the titles of articles, **142**

Pronunciation Key

ă	bat	ô	all
ā	ape	oi	toy
âr	**air**	ou	shout
ä	father	o͝o	book
ĕ	let	o͞o	moon
ē	**ea**sy	ŭ	nut
ĭ	if	ûr	circle
ī	lie	ə	**a**go
îr	**dear**	ər	moth**er**
ŏ	lot	′	primary stress
ō	go	′	secondary stress

heat (hēt) *n.* the movement of energy that makes things warmer, **102**

herbivores (hûr′bə vôrz′ *or* ûr′bə vôrz′) *n.* animals that eat only plants, **47**

hide (hīd) *v.* make hard to find, **43**

hill (hĭl) *n.* land that is higher than other land, **65**

humus (hyo͞o′məs) *n.* the part of soil made up of dead plants and animals, **58**

hurricanes (hûr′ĭ kānz′ *or* hŭr′ĭ kānz′) *n.* strong ocean storms, **87**

hypothesis (hī pŏth′ĭ sĭs) *n.* a possible answer or explanation, **133**

I

illustrations (ĭl′ə strā′shənz) *n.* drawings used to explain things, **153**

index (ĭn′dĕks′) *n.* a list of topics in the back of a book, **149**

inference (ĭn′fər əns) *n.* a conclusion made by putting together what you know and what you read, **164**

insects (ĭn′sĕkts′) *n.* small animals that have six legs and no backbone, **41**

instructions (ĭn strŭk′shənz) *n.* directions or orders, **194**

Internet (ĭn′tər nĕt′) *n.* a fast way to get information, **144**

iron (ī′ərn) *n.* a type of metal that magnets attract, **118**

K

key words (kē′ wûrdz′) *n.* words related to your topic that you use to search the Internet, **145**

kinds (kīndz) *n.* groups of one sort of thing, **24**

L

lake (lāk) *n.* a body of water with land all around it, **67**

land (lănd) *n.* the part of Earth's surface that is not under water, **39**

landforms (lănd′fôrmz′) *n.* ways Earth's land is shaped, **64**

languages (lăng′gwĭj əz) *n.* the words that groups of people use to talk and write, **180**

leaves (lēvz) *n.* the flat, green parts of a plant that stick out from the stem, **22**

lever (lĕv′ər *or* lē′vər) *n.* a bar that is used to move or lift something, **117**

life cycle (līf sī′kəl) *n.* the changes animals and plants go through as they grow, **50**

light (līt) *n.* a kind of energy that people use to see things, **104**

lightning (līt′nĭng) *n.* a flash of light in the sky during a thunderstorm, **86**

link (lĭngk) *n.* something on a Web site that you click on to go to another Web site, **145**

liquid (lĭk′wĭd) *n.* the state of matter that takes the shape of whatever space it is put in, **96**

live (lĭv) *v.* stay alive; survive, **18**

living (lĭv′ĭng) *adj.* able to change and grow, **18**

lungs (lŭngz) *n.* the parts in an animal's chest that help it breathe, **35**

M

magnet (măg′nĭt) *n.* an object that attracts certain metals, such as iron, **118**

main idea (mān′ ī dē′ə) *n.* the most important part of something, **160, 187, 188**

mammals (măm′əlz) *n.* warm-blooded animals that have a backbone and fur or hair, **35**

mass (măs) *n.* the amount of matter in an object, **93**

materials (mə tîr′ē əlz) *n.* things or substances you use in an experiment, **195**

matter (măt′ər) *n.* anything that takes up space, **92**

measure (mĕzh′ər) *v.* find out the amount of something, **128**

melt (mĕlt) *v.* become liquid, **98**

metal (mĕt′l) *n.* material that is shiny, hard, and conducts heat, **103**

methods (mĕth′ədz) *n.* plans of action, **132**

mind (mīnd) *n.* brain; the part of a person that thinks, **166**

minerals (mĭn′ər əlz) *n.* solid, nonliving substances that make up rocks, **57**

molds (mōldz) *n.* things that form when something soft like mud is pressed into the shape of something else, **62**

monitor (mŏn′ĭ tər) *v.* check, **170**

Moon (mo͞on) *n.* a large, round form that goes around Earth, **74**

motion (mō′shən) *n.* movement, **108**

mountain (moun′tən) *n.* the tallest landform, **64**

Pronunciation Key

ă	bat	ô	all
ā	ape	oi	toy
âr	**air**	ou	sh**ou**t
ä	father	o͝o	book
ĕ	let	o͞o	moon
ē	**ea**sy	ŭ	nut
ĭ	if	ûr	circle
ī	lie	ə	ago
îr	d**ear**	ər	moth**er**
ŏ	lot	′	primary stress
ō	go	′	secondary stress

N

nature (nā′chər) *n.* Earth and all living and nonliving things, **56**

needs (nēdz) *n.* things that are important for life, **28**

nonliving (nŏn′lĭv′ĭng) *adj.* not alive; not able to grow, **19**

notes (nōts) *n.* things that are written down to help remember information, **184**

O

observe (əb zûrv′) *v.* look closely at, **126**

ocean (ō′shən) *n.* a large body of salt water, **66**

omnivores (ŏm′nə vôrz′ *or* ŏm′nə vōrz′) *n.* animals that eat both plants and meat, **47**

orbit (ôr′bĭt) v. move around something in a path shaped like a circle, **78**

organize (ôr′gə nīz′) v. put things in a way so that they are easy to find and understand, **140, 186**

outline (out′līn′) n. a short, written plan of what you are going to write or say later, **186**

P

parts (pärts) n. pieces, **22**

paths (păths or päths) n. the directions something moves in, **109**

patterns (păt′ərnz) n. things repeated in order or relationships between things, **127**

pause (pôz) v. stop, **168**

photographs (fō′tə grăfs′) n. pictures taken with a camera that show real people, places, or things, **153**

pictures (pĭk′chərz) n. a way to communicate without words; drawings or photographs, **130, 142, 158**

pitch (pĭch) n. how high or low something sounds, **107**

plain (plān) n. a wide area of flat land, **65**

planets (plăn′ĭts) n. large, round forms that go around the Sun, **79**

plants (plănts) n. living things, such as trees or flowers, **18**

pollution (pə lōō′shən) n. waste in the environment that causes the air, water, and land to be dirty, **68**

precipitation (prĭ sĭp′ĭ tā′shən) n. water that falls back to Earth, **85**

predator (prĕd′ə tər) n. an animal that eats another animal, **49**

predict (prĭ dĭkt′) v. use what is known or observed to say what will happen, **129, 158**

prefix (prē′fĭks′) n. a group of letters at the start of a word, **178**

preview (prē′vyōō′) v. look ahead, **143**

prey (prā) n. an animal that a predator eats, **49**

producers (prə dōō′sərz or prə dyōō′sərz) n. living things that make their own food, **46**

properties (prŏp′ər tēz) n. special qualities or characteristics that describe things, **93**

pull (pŏŏl) v. use force on something so it moves closer, **110**

pulley (pŏŏl′ē) n. a wheel with a rope around it that is used to lift and lower something, **116**

purpose (pûr′pəs) n. a goal or reason to do something, **141**

push (po͝osh) *v.* use force against something so it moves, **110**

Q

questions (kwĕs′chənz) *n.* things you ask if you want answers, **124, 168**

R

rain (rān) *n.* water that falls from clouds, **81**

rain forest (rān′ fôr′ĭst *or* rān′ fŏr′ĭst) *n.* a forest habitat with lots of rain, **32**

rain gauge (rān′ gāj′) *n.* a tool that measures the rain, **83**

recycle (rē sī′kəl) *v.* break down to use again, **71**

reduce (rĭ dōōs′ *or* rĭ dyōōs′) *v.* use less, **70**

reflect (rĭ flĕkt′) *v.* bounce back, **105**

report (rĭ pôrt′ *or* rĭ pōrt′) *n.* a paper about what was learned, **188**

reptiles (rĕp′tīlz′ *or* rĕp′tĭlz) *n.* cold-blooded animals that have a backbone, **38**

reuse (rē yōōz′) *v.* use something again, **71**

revolve (rĭ vŏlv′) *v.* move around something in a circle, **76**

river (rĭv′ər) *n.* a body of water that moves, **67**

Pronunciation Key

ă	bat	ô	all
ā	ape	oi	toy
âr	**air**	ou	shout
ä	father	ō͝o	book
ĕ	let	ōō	moon
ē	**ea**sy	ŭ	nut
ĭ	if	ûr	circle
ī	lie	ə	ago
îr	**dear**	ər	moth**er**
ŏ	lot	′	primary stress
ō	go	′	secondary stress

rocks (rŏks) *n.* solid forms that are made up of minerals and found in nature, **56**

roots (rōōts *or* rō͝ ots) *n.* the parts of a plant that go into the soil, **22**

rotate (rō′tāt) *v.* spin, **75**

ruler (rōō′lər) *n.* a tool that measures how long something is, **192**

S

salt water (sôlt′ wô′tər *or* sôlt′ wŏt′ər) *n.* water that you cannot drink; most of Earth's water, **66**

sand (sănd) *n.* small pieces of rock that feel rough, **58**

scales (skālz) *n.* parts that cover the bodies of fish and reptiles, **37**

scientists (sī′ən tĭsts) *n.* people who study the natural world, **124**

screw (skrōō) *n.* a simple machine that is turned to hold things together, **116**

search (sûrch) *v.* look for, **144**

season (sē′zən) *n.* a time of year, **77**

seed (sēd) *n.* something that makes new plants, **24**, **50**

seedling (sēd′lĭng) *n.* a young plant that grows from a seed, **51**

senses (sĕns′əz) *n.* the five ways you take in information about the things around you, **126**

shadow (shăd′ō) *n.* the dark area you see when an object blocks the path of light, **105**

shape (shāp) *n.* the form of something or the way it looks, **95**

shells (shĕlz) *n.* parts of some animals that keep their insides safe, **40**

similar (sĭm′ə lər) *adj.* almost the same as something else, **180**

simple machines (sĭm′pəl mə shēnz′) *n.* tools that help us do work, **116**

skills (skĭlz) *n.* some things you can do, **125**

slow (slō) *v.* make something move less quickly, **114**

snow (snō) *n.* ice or water crystals that fall from clouds, **81**

soil (soil) *n.* dirt, **21**, **58**

solar (sō′lər) *adj.* coming from the Sun, **101**

solar system (sō′lər sĭs′təm) *n.* the Sun and all the objects that orbit it, **78**

solid (sŏl′ĭd) *n.* the state of matter that has a defined shape, like ice cubes, **95**

sort (sôrt) *v.* put into groups by a characteristic like size, color, or shape, **127**

sounds (soundz) *n.* things that can be heard; noises caused by vibrations, **106**

sources (sôrs′əs *or* sōrs′əs) *n.* the places where things come from, **101**, **185**

space (spās) *n.* room, **92**

speeds (spēdz) *n.* how fast things move, **109**

spills (spĭlz) *n.* liquid that has fallen on the ground, **195**

star (stär) *n.* something in the sky that gives off its own light, **73**

steam (stēm) *n.* very hot water that is a gas, **99**

stems (stĕmz) *n.* the main parts of plants that hold up the leaves and flowers, **22**

stop (stŏp) *v.* make something stay in one place; keep something from moving, **114**

stopwatch (stŏp′wŏch′) *n.* a tool that measures time, **193**

store (stôr) v. keep, **42**

streams (strēmz) n. small rivers, **67**

suffix (sŭf′ĭks) n. a group of letters at the end of a word, **178**

summarize (sŭm′ə rīz′) v. say only the most important ideas, **162**

summary (sŭm′ə rē) n. a few sentences about the important ideas in a text, **162, 184**

Sun (sŭn) n. the closest star to Earth, **72**

survive (sər vīv′) v. stay alive; live, **20**

T

table of contents (tā′bəl ŭv kŏn′tĕnts′) n. the part of a book that names the units and chapters in order, **147**

technology (tĕk nŏl′ə jē) n. useful tools that were made by scientists applying science ideas, **120**

temperature (tĕm′pər ə chŏŏr′ or tĕm′pər ə chər′ or tĕm′prə chŏŏr′ or tĕm′prə chər′) n. a measure of how hot or cold something is, **38, 83**

terms to know (tûrmz′ tĕ nō′) n. in this textbook, words in dark print or bold, **152**

textbook (tĕkst′bŏŏk′) n. a book that you read to help you learn, **140**

Glossary

Pronunciation Key

ă	bat	ô	all
ā	ape	oi	toy
âr	air	ou	shout
ä	father	ŏŏ	book
ĕ	let	ōō	moon
ē	easy	ŭ	nut
ĭ	if	ûr	circle
ī	lie	ə	ago
îr	dear	ər	mother
ŏ	lot	′	primary stress
ō	go	′	secondary stress

thermometer (thər mŏm′ĭ tər) n. a tool that measures the temperature, **83**

threatened (thrĕt′nd) adj. showing signs or warnings that a living thing will be in danger of not surviving soon, **44**

thunder (thŭn′dər) n. the loud noise caused by lightning during a thunderstorm, **86**

thunderstorm (thŭn′dər stôrm′) n. a strong storm with rain, lightning, and thunder, **86**

tilt (tĭlt) v. slope or slant, **77**

title (tīt′l) n. words at the top of a page that tell what the rest of the page is about, **151, 158, 188**

tools (tōōlz) n. things you use that help you do things, **192**

topic (tŏp′ĭk) n. what something is about, **140, 187**

tornadoes (tôr nā′dōz) *n.* strong wind storms that spin, **88**

toward (tôrd *or* tōrd *or* tə wôrd′) *adj.* in the direction of, **112**

tropical (trŏp′ĭ kəl) *adj.* very warm, **32**

U

understand (ŭn′dər stănd′) *v.* get the meaning of something, **170**

units (yo͞o′nĭts) *n.* parts of textbooks that name big topics, **140, 147**

V

valleys (văl′ēz) *n.* low, flat areas of land between hills or mountains, **65**

vapor (vā′pər) *n.* tiny drops of liquid that float in the air, **84**

vibrations (vī brā′shənz) *n.* movements caused when things move back and forth, **106**

visualize (vĭzh′o͞o ə līz′) *v.* make a picture of something in your mind, **166**

volume (vŏl′yo͞om *or* vŏl′yəm) *n.* how loud or soft something sounds, **107**

W

warm-blooded (wôrm′blŭd′ĭd) *adj.* adapted to keep a constant body temperature, **35**

wash (wŏsh *or* wôsh) *v.* make clean, **195**

waste (wāst) *n.* things that are left over or not needed; things that are thrown away, **70**

water cycle (wô′tər sī′kəl *or* wôt′ər sī′kəl) *n.* the movement of Earth's water from the ground to the air, and back to the ground, **84**

weather vane (wĕth′ər vān) *n.* a tool that measures wind direction, **83**

weather (wĕth′ər) *n.* what conditions are like outside, **80**

weathering (wĕth′ər ĭng) *n.* the breaking down of landforms by the Sun, water, and wind, **61**

Web site (wĕb′ sīt) *n.* a page on the Internet that has information about different topics, **145**

wedge (wĕj) *n.* a simple machine used to separate two things, **117**

wind (wĭnd) *n.* air that moves, **81**

wings (wĭngz) *n.* the parts of a bird that help it fly, **36**

words (wûrdz) *n.* the things you say or write to communicate, **130**

work (wûrk) *n.* when you use force to make something move, **116**

Art Credits

Burgandy Beam, p. **125** *top right, top left, middle, bottom right, bottom left;* Linda Bittner, pp. **48–49**; Anne Marie Boley, p. **23**; Dan Bridy, p. **101** *top right, top left, bottom right, bottom left;* Barbara Cousins, pp. **34, 150–151, 152**; Jeff Grunewald, pp. **72, 75**; George Hamblin, pp. **20, 64–65, 179**; Janet Skiles, p. **61** *top right, top left, bottom right, bottom left;* Toby Williams, pp. **84–85, 104**.

Photo Credits

Cover: ©Gary Gay/Getty Images, *right;* ©Stocktrek/age footstock, *bottom middle;* U.S. Geological Survey, HVO, *bottom left;* ©Comstock Images/PunchStock, *top;* Michelle D. Bridwell/PhotoEdit Inc., *bottom left;* ©Shutterstock Inc., *top right, top left, bottom right:* **cover front and back.**

©Ableimages/Getty Images, pp. **190–191**; ©Age Fotostock, pp. **4, 18, 19, 21, 96** *top,* **97** *middle,* **103, 105** *bottom left,* **111** *top,* **147** *top left,* **194** *bottom,* **195** *top;* ©Alamy, p. **193** *top;* ©Jacques Alexandre/Getty Images, p. **100** *left;* ©Bill Aron/PhotoEdit Inc., pp. **86, 112**; ©BananaStock/PunchStock, p. **92**; ©Dan Bigelow/Getty Images, p. **124**; ©Brand X Pictures/PunchStock, pp. **52, 99** *bottom left,* **178** *top;* ©Burke Triolo Productions/Getty Images, p. **127** *top left;* ©Alan and Sandy Carey/Getty Images, p. **36**; ©Cartesia/Getty Images, p. **66**; ©Myrleen Cate/PhotoEdit Inc., p. **165**; Cleo Photography/PhotoEdit Inc., p. **167** *left;* ©Comstock Images/Alamy,

p. **178** *bottom;* ©Comstock Images/PictureQuest, p. **40** *top left;* ©Comstock Images/PunchStock, p. **110** *top;* ©Corbis, pp. **22, 27** *bottom,* **29, 33** *top left,* **38, 39** *bottom,* **50** *right,* **51** *top, right, left, bottom,* **54–55, 140** *right,* **173** *left, right,* **184**; ©Corbis/Punchstock, pp. **13** *top,* **117** *top;* ©Creatas/Jupiter Images, p. **192** *bottom;* ©Creatas/PunchStock, pp. **45** *middle left,* **47** *middle;* ©C.Squared/Getty Images, p. **193** *bottom;* ©Bob Daemmrich/PhotoEdit Inc., p. **69** *top;* ©Phil Degginger/Carnegie Museum/Alamy, p. **162**; ©Digital Vision/Getty Images, p. **40** *bottom;* ©Digital Vision/PunchStock, pp. **25** *right, left,* **26, 32** *right, left,* **33** *bottom right,* **35**; ©Terry Donnelly/Getty Images, pp. **31, 33** *top right;* ©Eclipse Studios, pp. **8, 143, 159**; ©Bob Elsdale/Getty Images, pp. **14–15**; ©Europhoto/Age Fotostock, p. **94**; ©Alberto Fernández/Age Fotostock, p. **68**; ©Hoby Finn/Getty Images, p. **126**; ©David Ficher/Getty Images, pp. **182–183**; ©Getty Images, pp. **30** *bottom,* **71** *bottom,* **95** *top,* **97** *left,* **105** *top right,* **107** *top right,* **108, 111** *bottom;* ©Bob Gibbons/Science Photo Library, p. **105** *top left;* ©Erin Hogan/Photodisc/Getty Images, p. **129** *right;* ©Image Source/PunchStock, pp. **47** *left,* **81** *top right;* ©Index Stock Imagery Inc., pp. **119** *right,* **138–139**; ©Ingram Publishing/Age Fotostock, p. **81** *top left;* ©Ingram Publishing/Alamy, pp. **121** *top right,* **156** *left;* ©iStock International Inc., pp. **40** *top right,* **46, 58–59, 63** *bottom,* **69** *middle, bottom,* **74** *left,* **88, 89, 96** *bottom,* **97** *right,* **98** *right, left,* **99** *bottom middle, bottom right,* **102** *bottom right, top right,* **106, 109** *middle, bottom,* **121** *bottom right,* **127** *top,* **128** *bottom,* **129** *left,* **130, 147** *bottom,* **148, 160, 170, 172, 179, 181**